FAMILY LIFE IN CHINA

China Today series

FAMILY LIFE IN CHINA ——

William R. Jankowiak & Robert L. Moore

polity

First published in 2017 by Polity Press

Polity Press
65 Bridge Street
Cambridge CB2 1UR, UK

Polity Press
350 Main Street
Malden, MA 02148, USA

ISBN-13: 978-0-7456-8554-0
ISBN-13: 978-0-7456-8555-7(pb)

A catalogue record for this book is available from the British Library.

Library of Congress Cataloging-in-Publication Data

Names: Jankowiak, William R., author. | Moore, Robert L., 1949- author.
Title: Family life in China / William R. Jankowiak, Robert L. Moore.
Description: Malden, MA : Polity Press, 2016. | Includes bibliographical references and index.
Identifiers: LCCN 2016013483 (print) | LCCN 2016027806 (ebook) | ISBN 9780745685540 (hardback) | ISBN 9780745685557 (pbk.) | ISBN 9780745685571 (Mobi) | ISBN 9780745685588 (Epub)
Subjects: LCSH: Families–China. | Marriage–China. | China–Social life and customs.
Classification: LCC HQ684 .J36 2016 (print) | LCC HQ684 (ebook) | DDC 306.850951–dc23
LC record available at https://lccn.loc.gov/2016013483

Typeset in 11.5 on 15 pt Adobe Jenson Pro
by Toppan Best-set Premedia Limited
Printed and bound in Great Britain by Clays Ltd, St. Ives PLC

For further information on Polity, visit our website:
politybooks.com

Contents

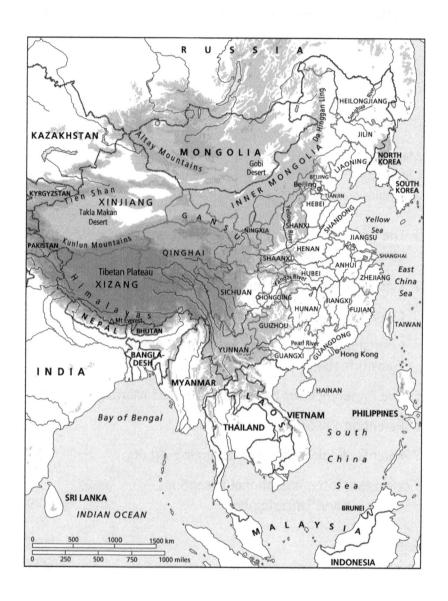

RUSSIA

KAZAKHSTAN

MONGOLIA

Altay Mountains

Gobi
Desert

INNER MONGOLIA

HEILONGJIANG

Songhua River

JILIN

Da Hinggan Ling

LIAONING

NORTH
KOREA

SOUTH
KOREA

KYRGYZSTAN

Tien Shan

XINJIANG

Takla Makan
Desert

GANSU

NINGXIA

BEIJING
Beijing

TIANJIN

HEBEI

Yellow River

SHANXI

SHANDONG

Yellow
Sea

JIANGSU

PAKISTAN

Kunlun Mountains

QINGHAI

HENAN

SHAANXI

ANHUI

SHANGHAI

Tibetan Plateau

XIZANG

Himalayas

SICHUAN

Yangzi River

HUBEI

CHONGQING

ZHEJIANG

East
China
Sea

NEPAL

△ Mt Everest

BHUTAN

HUNAN

JIANGXI

FUJIAN

TAIWAN

GUIZHOU

BANGLA-
DESH

INDIA

MYANMAR

YUNNAN

Pearl River

GUANGXI

GUANGDONG

Hong Kong

HAINAN

Bay of Bengal

LAOS

VIETNAM

PHILIPPINES

THAILAND

South

China

Sea

SRI LANKA

INDIAN OCEAN

BRUNEI

MALAYSIA

INDONESIA

0	500	1000	1500 km
0	250	500	750	1000 miles

Chronology

1894–95	First Sino-Japanese War
1911	Fall of the Qing dynasty
1912	Republic of China established under Sun Yat-sen
1927	Split between Nationalists (KMT) and Communists (CCP); civil war begins
1934–1935	CCP under Mao Zedong evades KMT in Long March
December 1937	Nanjing Massacre
1937–1945	Second Sino-Japanese War
1945–1949	Civil war between KMT and CCP resumes
October 1949	KMT retreats to Taiwan; Mao founds People's Republic of China (PRC)
1950–1953	Korean War
1953–1957	First Five-Year Plan; PRC adopts Soviet-style economic planning
1954	First constitution of the PRC and first meeting of the National People's Congress
1956–1957	Hundred Flowers Movement, a brief period of open political debate
1957	Anti-Rightist Movement
1958–1960	Great Leap Forward, an effort to transform China through rapid industrialization and collectivization

March 1959	Tibetan Uprising in Lhasa; Dalai Lama flees to India
1959–1961	Three Hard Years, widespread famine with tens of millions of deaths
1960	Sino-Soviet split
1962	Sino-Indian War
October 1964	First PRC atomic bomb detonation
1966–1976	Great Proletarian Cultural Revolution; Mao reasserts power
February 1972	President Richard Nixon visits China; 'Shanghai Communiqué' pledges to normalize U.S.-China relations
September 1976	Death of Mao Zedong
October 1976	Ultra-Leftist Gang of Four arrested and sentenced
December 1978	Deng Xiaoping assumes power; launches Four Modernizations and economic reforms
1978	One-child family planning policy introduced
1979	U.S. and China establish formal diplomatic ties; Deng Xiaoping visits Washington
1979	PRC invades Vietnam
1982	Census reports PRC population at more than one billion
December 1984	Margaret Thatcher co-signs Sino-British Joint Declaration agreeing to return Hong Kong to China in 1997
1989	Tiananmen Square protests culminate in June 4 military crack-down
1992	Deng Xiaoping's Southern Inspection Tour re-energizes economic reforms
1993–2002	Jiang Zemin is president of PRC, continues economic growth agenda

November 2001	WTO accepts China as member
2002–2012	Hu Jintao, General-Secretary CCP (and President of PRC from 2003)
2002–2003	SARS outbreak concentrated in PRC and Hong Kong
2006	PRC supplants U.S. as largest CO_2 emitter
August 2008	Summer Olympic Games in Beijing
2010	Shanghai World Exposition
2012	Xi Jinping appointed General-Secretary of the CCP (and President of PRC from 2013)

Acknowledgements

This project grew out of our long-term collaboration that resulted in various co-authored papers. Research for this project was supported in part by the Critchfield Fund and the George and Maeching Kao Fund for Chinese Scholarship at Rollins College.

We are most grateful to the staff at Polity Press overseeing the manuscript as it moved from design stage to production. We especially want to thank executive editor Emma Longstaff for first suggesting the topic, Jonathan Skerrett and Neil de Cort for their excellent advice and continuous attention to detail, which helped so much in making sure we met our target date for publication.

We would also like to call out and acknowledge support of Thomas Paladino who served as our ad hoc editor and provided advice and editing skills on several of the chapters. The numerous trips to Boston were well worth the finished product. In addition, we would like to thank Gene Anderson, Tami Blumenfield, Don Brown, Susan Brownell, Robert Carson, Myron Cohen, Goncalo dos Santos, Shanshan Du, Vanessa Fong, Tom Gregor, Stevan Harrell, Barry Hewett, Bonnie Hewlett, David Kronenfeld, Xuan Li, Melvyn Goldstein, Stephanie Sang, Alice Schlegel, Ray Scupin, Chuang-kang Shih, Charles Stafford, Yuzhu Sun, James Watson, Rubie Watson, Li Wei, Arthur Wolf, Yunxiang Yan, Yusheng Yao, Wenxian Zhang, Chang Zhao and two anonymous reviewers for their earlier research and analysis, which helped structure and guide our synthesis. We would also like to express our appreciation for the support offered by the ever patient and understanding members of our families: Sadie Hinson, Darla Moore, Grace Moore and Tyler Schimmelfing.

1 | The Chinese Family: Enduring Ideals and Changing Realities

> The Master said, If for the whole three years of mourning a son manages to carry on the household exactly as in his father's day, then he is a good son indeed.
>
> (*The Analects*, Confucius, trans. Waley 1938: 106)

THE SWAIN'S DILEMMA

In the great, sprawling Qing dynasty novel *The Dream of Red Mansions*, the central character, a young man named Baoyu, is faced with a dilemma: which lady shall he marry? The exquisitely lovely and delicate Black Jade, or the equally beautiful, but more worldly and pragmatic, Precious Virtue? His parents have settled on Precious Virtue as the most appropriate bride for their son, but he winds up falling in love with Black Jade. Both of these potential brides for Baoyu, by the way, are his first cousins.

First-cousin marriage was not unusual among elites of eighteenth-century China, the setting of *The Dream of Red Mansions*. Nor was it unusual in eighteenth-century Europe—or all that unusual in twentieth-century USA (Ottenheimer 1996), for that matter. But a distinction that Baoyu's family insists on, a distinction that reflects a longstanding principle of distinctly Chinese kinship, is the prohibition of marriage to *patrilineal* first cousins, that is, cousins related through one's father's brother. Welcoming Spring was, in fact, just such a first cousin to Baoyu, but marriage to her was as starkly prohibited as would be marriage to his own sister. Though Welcoming Spring is also a great beauty, nobody so much as hints at the possibility of her marrying Baoyu. Such a thing would be simply unthinkable.

In addition to the patrilineal principle, another issue brought forward by Baoyu's dilemma is parental control over marriages in traditional China. In the dramatic wedding scene near the end of *The Dream of Red Mansions*, Baoyu is led toward the sedan chair wherein the cousin his parents have selected for him waits, her face concealed behind a heavy red veil. But which maiden have they selected? The frail and gentle Black Jade, whom they know their son is mad about, or the capable and knowing cousin whom they have long favored: Precious Virtue.

Here too an enduring Chinese kinship principle comes into play: the idea that parents are in the best position to choose a wife for their son (or a husband for their daughter). Furthermore, by virtue of Confucian ethics, parents or other elders in the family have an undisputed right and obligation to make this selection.

These ideals—patrilineality and the right of elders to arrange their children's marriages—have undergone a number of transformations since the fall of China's last dynasty early in the twentieth century. But the hold that these ideals have on the thinking of contemporary Chinese has not entirely vanished. What role does the memory of the traditional Confucian family play in the lives of Chinese today? The answer to this question cannot be provided in a phrase or even a paragraph, but it is our hope that the historical and ethnographic overview that we present here will provide some answers, along with ideas for ways to pursue further investigations on this topic.

THE FAMILY AS ADAPTIVE INSTITUTION

The family, in view of the benefits it provides for its members, is generally regarded as a positive institution, even a necessary one.

Nevertheless, there has been a longstanding tendency among Western sociologists to view families in light of the problems often associated with them, problems like marginalization, gender discrimination, and child abuse. Differences in behavior linked to differences in social class have also drawn the attention of social scientists. Class differences are often cited as variables affecting rates of extramarital sexual relationships, the tendency to give birth to children outside of marriage, or the likelihood that marriages will end in divorce. These, of course, are all significant issues, but our goal here is to view the Chinese family not so much as a lens through which social problems may be viewed, but as an ever-changing and relatively adaptable institution which, over the past hundred years or so has undergone a series of dramatic adjustments in response to wider social changes.

CORE FEATURES

The Chinese family has displayed a variety of forms, functions, and relationship dynamics since the end of the Qing dynasty in 1911. Regional differences, urban vs. rural environments, and various other factors have resulted in variations in family organization, but these variations always respond to both traditional and officially sponsored ideals that make these forms identifiable as "Chinese." Before the establishment of the People's Republic of China (PRC) in 1949, the Chinese family was an economic, political, and jural unit. It rested on the assumption that males were central to its very existence; inheritance, both material and conceptual, was reckoned through males. The Chinese family was patrilineal. One's mother's relatives may have been emotionally significant, but power and, ideally, loyalty belonged to one's father's kin. Reinforcing this principle was the custom of virilocal marriage, that is, marriage in which a bride leaves her own natal family and joins her husband's. And finally, the traditional family was patriarchal, that is, power was presumed to be in the hands of men.

Furthermore, family elders were expected to have authority over younger members. These principles—patrilineality, virilocality, patriarchy, and deference to elders—underlay what is commonly referred to as the Confucian family, a family in which elderly males held most of the authority.

HISTORICAL CHANGES: AN OVERVIEW

With the creation of the PRC, socialist policies that created the *hukou* (household registration) system reinforced profound differences between rural and urban families, differences that had already existed to some extent. Cities became, more than ever, the centers of industry, commerce, and political governance, while rural areas, where 80 percent of the Chinese population resided in 1949, engaged primarily in agriculture. In response to these institutional changes, Chinese families began to diverge markedly along urban-rural lines. Rural Chinese families continued, more or less, the patriarchal tradition whereby parents arranged marriages, women were consigned to their status as the "inferior" gender, and pressures were placed on them to, above all, procreate sons. In contrast, the urban areas were organized around work units (*danwei*) that controlled individuals' employment and place of residence. In many ways, the state-sponsored *danwei* replaced the lineage and family in its role as provider of resources and cultural enforcer to its individual members. In the work unit–dominated era (from the 1950s to the 1990s), urban families typically followed a neolocal residence pattern. That is, wife and husband established a new residence rather than seeing the wife move in with the husband's family as had been the pattern in the past. Along with neolocal residence came a kind of de facto bilateral descent system, in which neither husband's nor wife's family took precedence in inheritance or family loyalty. To a large extent, the state initiated policies that wound up sweeping away the positions of authority previously held by older males in urban families.

REFORM ERA

Following the death of Mao Zedong in 1976, China underwent a series of reforms that once again reshaped the family. In post-reform China (from about 1980 to the present) the work units were weakened and families, which during the 1970s had already been pressured to limit their size were, after 1979, legally obligated to restrict themselves to only one child. All of these policies were set forward with the idea of modernizing and enriching China. Certainly this goal is now being achieved at a remarkable rate, though the changes that the Chinese family is being forced to undergo are still under study and no firm consensus has been reached as to what final form or forms the family will take.

VARIATIONS AND CYCLICAL VARIETIES

The term "Chinese family" serves as an umbrella term for an array of structures. In Chinese families today, individuals go through different stages of the life cycle, usually including marriage, parenting, and old age. Each of these life stages entails a different approach to identity with different expectations, rights, and responsibilities.

The rapidity with which the Chinese family has undergone change, particularly over the past few decades, is remarkable. Of course, this change has come largely in the context of, and in response to, changes in Chinese society at large. This dramatic series of changes in contemporary China presents us with an extraordinary opportunity to explore questions concerning change and the family in general. We might ask, for example, whether or not there is a kind of convergence with family systems in other societies, or if Chinese history and culture mediate change in such a way as to make them unique. Is the Chinese family today becoming an institution all but indistinguishable from the family in the United Kingdom or the United States? Or does it retain long-held values and behavioral patterns that make it distinct and different from families in the West?

Western scholarship has emphasized the transformation of Chinese society, and in doing so has at times neglected the forces of cultural continuity. This is especially so in studies where the very definition of "the family" has long posed a problem for scholars, both Western and Chinese. The variations in the Chinese family's social organization and customary practices, both past and present, pose a number of challenges due to their complexity. Adaptations to regional economic opportunities, the varying restrictions posed by official policy, and sometimes significantly different ethnic backgrounds have produced a dazzling mosaic of forms and behaviors. The richness in family forms has, for the people of China, created ambivalence concerning which behaviors can now be considered proper and which improper. This ambivalence is most acutely experienced in the way individuals understand the family as a cultural ideal and attempt to adjust to their ideal as they experience their own family as a living entity.

PAST SCHOLARSHIP ON FAMILY AND LINEAGE

Brandtstädter and Santos (2009) have argued that the theoretical perspectives of individual scholars tend to shape the way they conceive of the Chinese family. Some ethnographers (such as Fei Xiaotong) have focused their efforts on recording rural lives without organizing their research in terms of any overarching theoretical framework. Fei's work was groundbreaking and insightful on the specifics of family life, but it did not provide an analytical overview of Chinese kinship systems or family structures. It was not until the 1970s when Myron

Cohen (1976) working first in Taiwan, then in the 1980s in northern China (2005), and Rubie and James Watson (2004) working in Hong Kong in the 1970s, provided more closely analyzed ethnographic data that resulted in more refined understandings of these systems. The Watsons revealed that the Man lineage, which was originally based in the rural New Territories of Hong Kong, had morphed by the late twentieth century into a global entity with branches both in rural Hong Kong and urban Europe. At about the same time, Parish and Whyte (1978) conducted the first major investigations of mainland rural social life, though their methodology was statistical rather than ethnographic. There have been fewer studies of urban families because the rural Chinese family was long believed to be the repository of tradition and therefore potentially more interesting than the city-dwelling households that Westerners imagined to be largely divorced from Chinese tradition. Davis and Harrell (1993) broke new ground in the study of reform-era families, finding a significant impact on family structure from socialist policies. This analysis went counter to an earlier, widely held modernization thesis that overlooked specific state policies as primary factors in shaping the urban family.

THE MAOIST ERA AND THE IMPACT OF THE STATE

Families typically adjust their patterns of behavior in response to changing political and economic circumstances. This means that there is seldom a single ideal type to which every family aspires to conform. Instead, there is a range of ideal types based partly on enduring traditions and partly on the demands of local conditions, which may be in flux (Davis and Harrell 1993). For most of China's history, the ideal family was the multigenerational joint family, wherein married brothers continued to live together as a unified economic and social unit with their parents and children. It was never easy to maintain such a family, particularly for those with limited resources. This ideal was undermined with China's post-1949 experimentation with Maoist socialism. At this time, Communist Party policies "reshaped the social landscape and introduced new features or possibilities (e.g., high age of marriage, elimination of polygamy and concubinage, reduced dowries and weakened corporate kin groups) into the reorganized Chinese family" (Davis and Harrell 1993:19). Following the death of Mao in 1976, the Reform Era introduced an entirely new social landscape to which families had to adapt. This era was marked in particular by the retreat of the government from its effort to organize domestic life and it "resulted in the return of many traditional features (e.g., precommunist festivals, bride price and lavish dowry, and joint family households) associated with the Chinese family" (Davis and Harrell 1993:20–21).

CHANGE: IN CHINA THE FAMILY IS A BIG FACTOR

In the years between 1949 and 1980, the Chinese family organization owed more to the enforcement of state policies than it did to the forces of industrialization and urbanization. The important role of state policy in shaping family dynamics makes the Chinese case an exception to the model offered by William Goode in his discussion of modernization. His thesis, that the primary forces reshaping family organization were urbanization and industrialization, is accurate as far as it goes, but in the case of mainland China there is more to this story. There has been a worldwide trend in which the extended family is replaced by the nuclear family; the kin group's influence declines and there is decreasing emphasis on marital transfers of wealth such as bride prices and dowries. Concomitant with these changes comes a loss in parental control over whom their children should marry. These factors reflect a growth in individual independence, and they are connected to the expansion of individual opportunities in the labor market. They amount in particular to a shift toward increased freedom in mate choice, the timing of marriage, and, finally, an increase in divorce rates. Seeing this pattern as a consequence of industrialization and urbanization may be valid for Western Europe (as well as for Hong Kong and Taiwan) but it is only partially true for mainland China, where an active and often aggressive state has a significant role in shaping citizens' everyday lives. In this environment, forceful, top-down policies brought about some of the changes that in other societies came along as part of broad social developments. For example, soon after the establishment of the PRC, state policies began to dismantle the power of lineages and clans, particularly in urban areas. The new marriage law, promulgated in 1950, undermined parents' control over their offsprings' courtship and mate choice, and men's control over their wives. Both of these changes resulted in enhanced opportunities for the development of conjugal affection and spousal loyalties.

PROPERTY AND PARENTAL POWER: IN THE PRC THE STATE CHANGES ALL

Goode's thesis is consistent with Jack Goody's emphasis on the importance of heritable property as a factor in shaping family decisions. (For a discussion of family and property, see Davis and Harrell 1993:6.) Goody argued that families with land tended to invest heavily in their children since they could give them an inheritance. However, families living within a state-sponsored collectively owned property unit were not in a position to offer their children a family inheritance. Davis and Harrell (1993:1) were the first to point out that the "elimination of most private property destroyed much of the economic motivation that had previously shaped family loyalties. And the frontal attack on ancestor worship and lineage organization struck at the cultural religious core of the extended family." Yet the reforms undeniably provided stability, at least in the early years of Maoism, and during this time more children survived to marry and more parents survived into old age than had been the case before 1949. State policies created the conditions conducive to the formation of larger multigenerational households that had extensive economic and social ties to kin. In effect, and contrary to Goode's materialistic thesis, Davis and Harrell (1993) point out that China's state power has been the creator of the contemporary family form.

ENHANCED POWER FOR WOMEN

Socialist policies also enhance China's longstanding social differentiation between rural and urban communities. These policies helped transform the PRC into a nation of two competing cultural universes: one in the cities, the other in the villages. They also forced the urban populace to rely on bureaucratic agencies, thereby weakening the traditional patrilineal and virilocal forms in favor of a more flexible system organized around the principles of neolocal residence and bilateral descent. Moreover, state policies provided expanded opportunities for urban women, who, unlike their rural counterparts, gained greater access to the labor force along with a salary that for many families proved crucial. On top of this, women in cities all over China for the first time had equal access to educational opportunities. These newly found resources of power enabled many women in the work-unit (*danwei*) era (1959–1990s) to achieve parity with men in family decisionmaking. These changes also served to enhance women's social standing generally, both within the domestic sphere and outside of it. Significantly, the Reform Era (from 1979 to the present), which has been characterized by a retreat of state policies, has not thereby seen a weakening of women's social standing within the family. The gains that women made in the Maoist era have not been lost in the Reform Era. This trend was bolstered by the increase in women's employment and the decrease in family size, which was further encouraged by the one-child policy of 1979. All of these things elevated the status of daughters in urban households, where they were often their parents' only child. This enhanced esteem has had some effect on marriages generally; urban females are often able to hold their own in interactions with their husbands.

TAIWAN AND MAINLAND

In a comparative study covering Taiwan and southeastern mainland China, Chu and Yu (2010) discovered a variety of changes that mark the family forms in these two regions. Some of the patterns their data reveal show a degree of similarity between Taiwan and mainland. For example, family size in both areas has fallen. On the mainland, family size shrank from a 1982 average of 4.36 to 3.45 by 2000. For Taiwan, family size steadily decreased from its 1961 high of 5.57 to 3.21 in 2003. Second, the average age for first marriage for both Taiwan and mainland China has steadily increased over the last fifty years. But Chu and Yu also uncovered some significant differences. For example, though age at marriage is rising in both regions, mainland couples still tend to marry at younger ages than those on Taiwan. Moreover, a significant proportion of people on the mainland still have their marriages arranged by professional matchmakers, a practice that has been all but abandoned on Taiwan.

PARADOX: OLD CULTURAL IDEALS, NEW CULTURAL REALITIES

There are a number of paradoxes characterizing China's families today, as well as Chinese society in general. The People's Republic of China, established under the leadership of the Chinese Communist Party (CCP) in 1949, has enjoyed a period of relative peace and increasing

prosperity that has lasted for almost seventy years. Though CCP policies from the outset were aimed at establishing collective consciousness
and collective institutions, they have often promoted individualism.
Furthermore, Communist Party reform inadvertently enabled for a
time the establishment of families that, more than in the immediate
past, resembled the Confucian-based ideal family.

This ideal family is multigenerational and is organized around
parental willingness to sacrifice for the sake of their dependents and
to make judicious investments of their resources for the long-term
advancement of the family's status (Davis and Harrell 1993). As we
will discuss below, however, the parent-offspring obligations implied
in these parental sacrifices are no longer the primary bases of emotional bonds today. At least they are not for a large proportion of
China's families.

The economic reforms that gained steam in the 1980s resulted in a
shift away from a redistributive system based on official rank and connections to one based mainly on class and adaptation to the new
market system (Whyte 2005). This shift has had consequences for the
organization of household property, as well as new ideals of intimacy,
decisions about fertility, and the care of kin. With all of these factors,
individual interests are coming prominently into play. We can see here
a directional shift that is consistent with Goody's thesis that bride
price and dowry should decline in significance in a redistributive
economy but can be expected to increase in value whenever private
property becomes more important. This is exactly what is now occurring in China.

There is no longer a consensus over what the preferred ideal actually
is, nor is there clear agreement on the proper motivation for the performance of family roles. Today, there are different voices that vary
across China and even within any given locale. Moreover, this complexity is generational—each age cohort having different understandings

and expectations about family interactions. This does not mean there are no patterns; there clearly are. But it does mean that familial patterns are as varied as they have always been throughout Chinese history.

Rather than a single family type, there are today multiple forms that range from the joint family to the stem family to the nuclear or conjugal family to the post-nuclear or multigenerational family. And as in the past, family members, at different stages in their lives, often live in different family types that range from conjugal (that is, only one married couple) to stem (two married couples in different generations live together) to joint (two or more married couples in the same generation).

Throughout late imperial China, the ideal family was one where all married brothers and their wives lived under one roof with the brothers' parents. It was a place where sons and their wives were expected to prosper together. The wives, according to the ideal, had all followed the virilocal residence rule and married into their husbands' family, their natal family having received a substantial bride price as part of the marriage settlement. In this ideal world, it was deemed essential that the family and not the individual was the stabilizing factor that served as the basis for the maintenance of social, cultural, economic, and personal well-being. In this milieu, actions that promoted family stability and continuity took precedence over other interests, and stability and continuity were closely associated with shared common property. Cohen (1995:65) noted that property is the family's foundation, the cornerstone that enables it to act as a corporate unit.

The Reform Era resulted in the end of collectivization and the return of the collectively held state land to the farmers. The state, in returning land to rural families, reintroduced the old incentive—private property—that Chinese farmers could once again use as a basis for a corporate or joint family. Cohen notes that in the pre-communist era, family property was always larger and more significant for life satisfaction than was individual property (Cohen 1995:65). Elders, for the most part, were able to use the benefits of having corporate family property to hold the family together. Married brothers, no matter how much they or their wives might have preferred conjugal living, were highly cognizant of the dangers that the pursuit of individual self-interests could bring about for the entire family (Cohen 1976). It was the wealth generated on the basis of commonly owned corporate property that kept the family together. Cohen further points out, however, that there was another factor that tended to pull married brothers apart. This was the desire of their wives (individuals who were usually born in different villages and had moved into their husband's parents' home) to live separate lives. Once she felt that her husband could support his family, a wife might well strive to break away from the large family, initiating a process that could result in the establishment of several separate conjugal units. This female strategy seemed to be most effective after the death of her husband's parents.

Cohen's mainland and Taiwan research reveals a paradox: the desire for privacy and independence results in the formation of an independent conjugal unit and, as such, represents the "modernization" of the Chinese family. On the other hand, wanting to form and maintain a unified family based on ownership of corporate property made economic sense, while upholding the belief that the joint family is the best family ideal (Cohen 1995:96). The Chinese government's efforts to move China away from an agrarian civilization into an urban one based on manufacturing, service, and professional development may render the current paradox moot. For the vast majority of Chinese citizens, the decision to live in a joint or conjugal family will be irrelevant. Something akin to a conjugal or post-conjugal family constituted by a married couple and perhaps a co-resident relative may be the only option, given the restrictions of urban housing in China today.

RITUALS AS DEVICES FOR FAMILY STABILITY

One of the ways stability was ensured in the past was through the performance of family rituals that highlighted the importance of belonging to a larger institution, whether extended family, lineage, or clan. This ideal of an enduring, multigenerational kin group was often not achieved, as explained above, due to each brother's wife tacitly, but relentlessly, trying to undermine family unity (Cohen 1976).

The resources available to an individual always played a part in determining how close to the ideal family a household could come. Most men born to extremely poor families would never marry, since they could not afford the bride price. For them, no continuance of their family line was in the cards. Instead they would live their lives out in their natal families. Other impoverished men could marry if they agreed to move into their wife's natal family and perhaps adopt her surname and even agree to have some or maybe even all of their children inherit their wife's surname as well. This was considered an extremely undesirable fate. Other men from impoverished households might have been obligated to marry an adopted "sister." This fate too, as Arthur Wolf (1995) documents, most men and women preferred to avoid.

Over the last fifty years mainland Chinese have had to confront a number of challenges. It would be incorrect to infer, however, that the intense transformation of the Chinese family only began under the Chinese Communist Party. Whyte and Parish's 1980s urban survey found that many of the domestic changes concerned with kinship obligations, conjugal duties, and parent-child interaction were already underway prior to the establishment of the People's Republic in 1949. Many of these changes, in other words, were gradual and not radical (Whyte and Parish 1984:191–92). In accordance with Goode's thesis, these changes have been unfolding in China's largest cities for over fifty years (Wu 1987). In this way some but not all of the changes in

Chinese families are typical of Goode's claim that there is a worldwide trend toward the establishment of nuclear or conjugal families that also entails a decline in fertility and decreasing power for senior members of kinship groups.

THE CONJUGAL FAMILY

Goode's study of individualized Western societies illustrates that the conjugal family with its intense emotional bond between husbands and wives has become the modern ideal (1970:9). To some extent, this ideal has taken root in China, but almost always incorporating some trace of the Confucian past. Among urban singletons' families, the intimate emotional bond between parents and children appears to be just as powerful as the conjugal bond between husbands and wives (Yan 2003). Even before the promulgation of China's one-child policy in 1979 (Whyte et al. 2015), single children had become the primary source of emotional investment and satisfaction for their parents (Fong 2004:125, 143). Moreover, emotional investment and intimacy go in both directions: children often seek emotional support and intimacy from their parents. The remembrance and recalling of parenting offers us a lens through which to glimpse the establishment and formation of the love-based relationship ties between urban Chinese youth and their parents. These changes can be seen in rural migrant families, urban families, and most recently, in the households of same-sex couples. In short, China today offers a kaleidoscope of family types, differing in composition, with reinterpretations of kinship bonds, of marriage, of childbearing expectations, of parenting, of intergenerational obligations, and of understandings of the nature of youth and emerging adulthood as well. In the following chapters we will highlight some of the more significant trends and changes that have shaped and are continuing to shape the Chinese family as a conceptual form and as a lived experience.

2 | Kinship, Friends, and the Multigenerational Family

The best family is one in which all sons with their wives live together in a large house. My four sons are planning to marry and they will all live around me in this old flat house where we will enjoy life together. (A sixty-four-year-old woman, from William Jankowiak's unpublished fileld notes)

For centuries the Chinese moral universe has been conceived of as an essentially family-based system, whose central features are the virtue of filial piety (*xiao*) and the familial duties surrounding ancestor worship (Santos 2006:275–333). The basis of society has traditionally been the multigenerational family, which ideally included five patrilineally linked generations. This moral universe predominated during the late Imperial era and even continued to endure throughout the Republican era, only ending with the establishment of the People's Republic of China in 1949. In this system, the father-son relationship was the primary moral axis, and it served, in many ways, as the fundamental ethical foundation not just for the family but for the Chinese social and political order as a whole. As ideals, the most important elements of this order were the following: 1) the centrality of the father-son bond, 2) emotional distance between husband and wife, 3) the obligation of each generation to produce numerous offspring, 4) the disinclination to recognize childhood as a distinct life stage, and 5) the authority of parents to instruct and command junior family members (Yan 2010:493).

This patrilineal and patriarchal ideal was beginning to lose ground during the waning years of the nineteenth century, and, following the May Fourth Movement launched in 1919, it suffered a number of new challenges that further weakened it. Then, after the Communist victory and establishment of the People's Republic of China, Marxist-based policies brought about dramatic changes to Chinese families that included in particular the undermining of the authority of the senior generation. Finally, some thirty years after the establishment of the PRC, the market reforms under Deng Xiaoping, in tandem with the one-child policy, further altered traditional familial forms, largely through the empowering of individuals, particularly young adult individuals. A moral order that had for centuries required deference and obedience from the young within the family, was gradually supplanted by one that encouraged the individualistic pursuit of meaning and significance in a newly emerging and rapidly changing social order. Perhaps the most striking change from the old patriarchal order to the new Reform Era family was the unprecedented positive evaluation of female children. Though it is not the case that every Chinese family longs to have a daughter, it is certainly true that, as of the beginning of the Reform Era, the perceived value of daughters has dramatically improved. Today, most urban families are perfectly happy to have their one child be a daughter and, in fact, there is a growing tendency among some to see daughters as preferable to sons in the long run, given their propensity to form strong emotional bonds with their parents, especially with their mothers (Fong 2004, Li 2014). The shift in familial expectations has resulted in the ideals of duty and obligation being largely replaced with the appreciation of positive emotion as the basis of family bonds (Jankowiak 2006, Yan 2003). Chinese society, since 1949, and especially since 1980, has been undergoing a cultural transformation that is reshaping not only the structural aspect of ordinary lives but also their cognitive, emotional, and ethical spheres. This transformation will have enduring significance for the people of China, and it offers those with an interest in China's future with an array of issues to consider.

A BRIEF OVERVIEW OF CHINESE KINSHIP RESEARCH

In studying Chinese kinship, scholars have often approached concepts in light of their own overriding theoretical interests. Chinese anthropologists trained in Western universities conducted some of the earliest ethnographic studies on Chinese village life (Harrell 2001). Many of these village-focused studies, like that of the influential Fei Xiaotong, were insightful and enlightening in their carefully observed detail, but they did not provide a theoretical overview of Chinese kinship and family life. It was not until Maurice Freedman's groundbreaking analyses of southern China's rural lineage organization that the field was presented with a powerful organizing model of Chinese kinship (Freedman 1966, 1970). Freedman's work was remarkable in that it was based not on ethnographic fieldwork but on data provided in written sources available to him as an armchair anthropologist. The theoretical forebears whose work helped Freedman organize his thinking were largely specialists on lineages in African societies. "Inspired by Meyer Fortes' essay on unilineal descent groups, Freedman defined patrilineal descent as a political-jural principle of intergenerational transmission of power and property which was more important than the principles of affinity" (Santos 2006:293).

For decades Freedman's classic lineage model remained the standard for discussing Chinese kinship as a descent system based on property held in common by lineage members. As Freedman's study emphasized, Chinese villages in the southern provinces of Guangdong and Fujian were often virtually coterminous with lineages, and, in fact, in many cases a village would be named for the lineage that founded it and whose members made up the bulk of its inhabitants. Such lineage villages could function as close corporate units favoring their members over outsiders. In effect, a village could be, under the authority of lineage elders, a readily mobilized unit whose male members were primed to defend its interests against all challengers. Freedman, in focusing his analyses on data from southeastern China, was unaware that most northern villages did not develop the elaborate lineage organizations so typical of the south. Furthermore, Freedman and his students, being influenced by the structural anthropology that dominated British theory at the time, were generally uninterested in exploring the emotional lives of the Chinese, whether north or south. He focused his analyses on the official, Confucian-based ideology and the ideal image of family and lineage that it entailed. He ignored private experiences and local practices, though, in his defense, the political restrictions on ethnographic research in the People's Republic at the time precluded a more nuanced fieldwork-based analysis. In any case, Freedman's structural model, despite its groundbreaking revelations, is now regarded as too restrictive and no longer adequate for understanding Chinese society and kinship (Brandtstädter and Santos 2009).

In place of Freedman's lineage paradigm, two alternative models of contemporary Chinese family social organization have emerged: the corporate model and the private-life model. The corporate model views the family primarily as an "economic entity composed of rational, self-interested members," and as "an organization characterized by a common budget, shared property, and a household economy that relies on a strict pooling of income" (Yan 2003: 70; Cohen 2005a). From this perspective, the Chinese family functions as the basic unit for the financial management of its members who organize their behavior toward advancing the economic interests of the family. Under the corporate model, the source of parental authority is the economic power that parents, especially fathers, have over their offspring. Myron

Cohen developed this model on the basis of his fieldwork first in a Hakka-speaking Taiwanese village, and later through his investigation of kinship in several northern Chinese villages. Cohen sees two primary developmental stages as inherent in the Chinese family. In the first stage, parents control their offspring mainly through the all-encompassing supervision of their children's development. As the children mature and assume more social responsibility, the family enters the second phase of its life cycle; with parents managing their children's life-orientations by guiding and, at times, demanding that their offspring engage in actions that benefit the family's economic interests (Cohen 1976:70).

Cohen, following Lang (1946), noted that the family, as a structural entity, typically went through a cyclical series of stages. A married couple with children, a conjugal family, can be taken as a starting point in this cycle. But once a son in the junior generation brings a wife into the household and with her procreates a child, this simple family becomes a stem family, that is, a three-generation patrilineal household. This cyclical process may continue as other sons marry and reproduce. Eventually, as other sons bring in wives and begin to build their own families, the household would then be considered a joint family: a family three generations deep in which more than one brother has brought in a wife. Should the parents die, the brothers, as long as they stayed together as a functioning unit, would be a fraternal joint family. Should the brothers in such a fraternal joint family divide into separate economic and residential units, what remains then will be a group of conjugal families, at which point the entire cycle may begin again with each of them (Cohen 1976).

Cohen's work casts the family as a corporate body, as did Freedman's analysis of Chinese lineages. But Cohen differs from Freedman by virtue of his emphasis on the agency of family members in the context of a patrilineal ideal. Though descent lies behind the decisions that individual family members make, their decisions reflect their understanding of their stake in the system, rather than submission to an all-encompassing, descent-based patrilineage. It is worth noting that the Taiwanese community where Cohen did his initial fieldwork is part of the general southeastern Chinese culture area on which Freedman's analysis focused.

The corporate model offers a powerful framework for exploring developmental shifts in the late imperial Chinese family. The model continues to hold value for understanding family variation, especially in southern Chinese village life. The ongoing shift away from rural to urban life has resulted, however, in greater prominence in enhancing individual life goals that are often separate from the interests of the family as a corporate entity. It is now common for Chinese family members to make life choices not out of economic necessity, nor with an ideal Confucian family system in mind, but in light of their personal aspirations that may include pursuit of material and emotional satisfaction. These aspects of the changing Chinese family are best highlighted through the private-life model.

Yunxiang Yan was one of the first researchers to notice the shift in life orientation toward more emphasis on the subjective or internal life of the individual. His research in a northern Chinese village found the family often functioned as a psychological rather than a structural or economic entity. Unlike families of traditional China, the typical rural family investigated by Yan has come to be seen, more than anything, as a "private haven" that serves primarily as an emotional center wherein individuals seek a sense of well-being (Yan 2003:9). Yan's private-life model highlights the varying interests and enterprises of the family's individual members, while the corporate model focused on the social roles that individuals were expected to fulfill over their life courses. While it isn't the case that affective ties were nonexistent or trivial in traditional families, their increasing importance makes them more worthy of attention today, as individuals act in light of personal goals more than was typical in the past.

Because family life is more fluid and less closed than the Chinese lineage model implies, individuals sometimes strive to establish and maintain rich social connections, that is, *guanxi*, outside the family. As we will discuss further below, these connections reflect individual initiative and are ego-centered rather than being oriented to a collective entity like the family (Kipnis 1997).

Rural life, then, is today as much about personal concerns as it is about accepting one's place within a corporate hierarchy. When viewed in light of the private life model, individuals can be seen as having "sensibilities, desires, sexual experiences, love crushes, aspirations to autonomy, privacy, and independence" (Santos 2006:331). This is not to deny the continuing pull of the structural features of the family that China's cultural underpinnings set forth, but only to say that individuals respond to a variety of factors in their behavior, only some of which correspond to the demands of family as an ideal form.

To a large extent, the policies of the Chinese Communist Party were responsible for the decline of the corporate family. But the Reform Era has seen further influences that pushed the family in the same direction. The gradual abandonment of the socialist work unit and the corresponding rise of private enterprise generated an environment in which private space became an important and ever-expanding feature of urban life (Lee 1998:23). In this setting, the private-life approach is well suited to probe the Chinese urban family as an institution that comprises a bundle of individual experiences and perspectives. Both corporate and private life perspectives offer informative approaches to an understanding of family life in China. Each has its place, though the rise of individualistic values in Chinese culture makes the latter particularly revealing about modern trends. Individuals will typically strive to uphold the interests of the family as a whole; there is for many, however, a certain wariness felt by individuals who are reluctant to be ensnared in a web of all-too-demanding interpersonal relationships (Yan 2003:6).

The contemporary urban Chinese family has become a fundamentally nuclear unit whose members are somewhat less interested in the family's status than their forebears were, but who seek above all a haven within which emotional satisfactions are sought (Gold 1985:671). The one-child policy, successfully implemented in major Chinese cities (modified in 2015 to allow for two children), further exacerbated this individualistic trend as many urbanites withdrew from government-driven "public movements" and instead channeled their "energy and emotion into bringing up one perfect child" (Gold 1985:671–72).

The private-life approach presents the family as a domain in which individuals face competing interests, respond to varied emotional bonds, and do so in light of nuanced ethical ideals rather than a rigid structural agenda. But where individualistic trends are on the rise, complexity and diversity are sure to be part of the story. Ellen Oxfeld's study of a Guangdong village in southeastern China finds that family-based ethical obligations continue to serve as a primary source of identity construction and status (Oxfeld 2010). Her research serves as a reminder of the diversity of the Chinese family from region to region and provides a qualification to studies like that of Yan (2003) in northeastern China, which, as we have seen, reveals the power that individualistic motives can have even in the face of the ideals of cultural tradition. It might best be said that the rise of individualism has occurred in many contexts within the PRC, but its impact varies from region to region. Both the private-life and corporate perspectives are useful for understanding the dramatic changes in Chinese society over the last two decades, as well as the increasing diversity that these changes have made more prominent. Both models allow for the exploration of the "subjectivity" of individual family members as it is manifested in "emotionality, desire, intimacy, privacy, individuality…and other forms of sociality" (2003:9). The two approaches differ mainly in their point of analytical emphasis. In the end, both approaches provide an accurate account of the Chinese family as structural units and as arenas where ongoing cultural and psychological transformations are voiced, debated, contested, managed, and, at times, resolved.

CHINESE KINSHIP: TRENDS AND FINDINGS

Chinese kinship can be seen as having two core features: a network of mutual help between households, and the concept of patrilineal descent that has particular force in certain symbolic contexts. These contexts include, for example, social orderings, and material gifts at such ritual events as funerals, marriages, and family photographs. Elements of the patrilineal system's survival can be seen in the granting of pride of place in the center for the elderly in family photographs, and the continued use of certain patrilineally based kin terms of address. Furthermore, it is still the custom for the groom's family (in first marriages) to pay for the wedding. But a number of other traditional features of the patrilineal system have been abandoned in favor of individuals' situational needs. For example, there is no rule today as to where the bride and groom should live after the wedding, at least for urban families. Most newlywed couples will find their own apartment, while others may live with the groom's or the bride's family, depending upon their needs and desires. It is, however, expected that the groom's family will eventually provide housing for the couple. In parts of rural China, a customary bias in favor of inheritance through the male line persists, especially when a daughter marries out. However, communist egalitarianism has resulted in urban patterns of inheritance where neither gender nor marital status determines one's share of heritable property. The decline in the importance of patrilineal descent also extends to naming practices. In the past, offspring ordinarily took their father's family name, despite the fact that their mother kept her own maiden name even after she was married. Today naming practices may include both paternal and maternal relations (Watson and Watson 2004).

Kinship can be seen as a burden as much as a source of benefits. An important reason for this is the new and increasingly diversified market economy in which parents, adult children, and other kin may work at different jobs, and may therefore have developed their own, individual-centered networks of friends. Each family member may have a unique support network, and so traditional dependence on one's own kin is reduced while reliance on friends in the workplace and elsewhere increases. The expansion of the market economy requires urbanites to pursue a broad-based strategy of social interaction that depends on forming relationships with both kin and non-kin. One informant from the city of Hohhot, when asked to make a distinction between kin and friends, said, "Friends are for mundane matters, family is for ritual affairs." In 1982 a twenty-eight-year-old female from the same city poignantly revealed, "We hide from our cousins but not from our friends." In this way, kin can be seen as in competition with "friends." In general, the "big family" (*da jia*) no longer exists as the dominant form of social organization in urban China. There are few occasions in which all siblings and siblings' children gather. These mainly include such important family events as weddings and funerals, or when a family member suddenly faces a serious illness.

Not only in China but also in the world generally, there has been an emerging pattern according to the way in which generations share or distribute resources. In the past the tendency was for parents to provide for offspring, but now there is something of a reverse of this. Parents are likely to be recipients of resources from their adult offspring. This pattern, with only a few modifications, is typical of intergenerational relations in urban China and is also found on Taiwan. Robert Marsh found that an intergenerational flow of help and resources from offspring to their parents was greater in 1991 than in 1963 (Marsh 1996:305). As always, broad patterns do not tell the complete story about this relationship. For example, one twenty-two-year-old man admitted that he never gave money to his parents, because, he said, "I need money to buy things and improve my life." In his case, he was aware that his parents did not need money. His case was typical of many prosperous families. Another anomaly can be seen in unmarried females in some financially secure households who routinely give a small sum of money to their parents as a symbolic statement of affection rather than out of any financial need on the parents' part.

Urban China's current affluence means that there is less need for parents to receive financial support from their offspring. But in cases where the parents have been laid off or are otherwise jobless, their teenage or young adult offspring are expected to help sustain them with regular monetary contributions. This shift in resource allocation has not diminished the intensity of affective bonds between children and parents. The depth of feeling between offspring and parents is likely to be as intense as it ever was, if not more intense in light of the new emphasis on affective bonds that characterize contemporary families.

The range of kinship bonds has been steadily shrinking in twentieth-century China. This means that few kin who are not members of one's nuclear family play important parts in one's life. However, the emotional pull of the family, however diminished in size this entity has become, continues to be quite strong. People continue to think of the family (*jia*) as the dominant metaphor with which to assist and evaluate one's progress through life. Social maturity and even, to an extent, psychological stability, are thought to be indicated by one's marital status and whether or not one has any offspring.

By the beginning of the twenty-first century, the government-imposed restrictions on birth resulted in most urban families having (at most) one child, and rural families rarely having more than two. The rural restriction allowed for a family to have a second child if the first one born to it were a girl. In fact, rural parents that had a daughter, or even, in some cases, two daughters, would typically try for another child in the hope that it would be a boy. In some cases, bribery or the use of *guanxi* obligations allowed for parents without a son to go beyond the two-child restriction that rural families were supposed to abide by. In other cases, a family would willingly pay the fine that resulted from their having a third child, if that child turned out to be the son they had anxiously hoped for. It is difficult to know if urban Chinese really wanted two children, but it is suggestive that urban members of minority ethnic groups (who were allowed to have two or more offspring) overwhelmingly chose to have only one (Jankowiak 1993). This implies that the state-imposed cultural ideal of one child has become, especially for urbanites, the new preferred ideal. Although China has now allowed for two children, the ideal of one child (or none) remains prominent in the PRC. Moreover, as Cohen points out, Taiwan and Hong Kong, without state-imposed restrictions, have the lowest fertility rates in the world.

The traditional ideal of a large family continues to affect the way parents categorize and instruct their children on how to address their playmates: the preferred idiom is to address each other with a fictive kinship term: brother or sister. For example, it is not uncommon to find children who are friends referring to one another as older brother (*ge*) and younger brother (*di*) or older sister (*jie*) and younger sister (*mei*). This pattern is often manifested whenever a child is asked about their relationship with a friend. They typically reply that "he or she is my older or younger brother or sister." When asked if the person is their real (*zhende*) brother or sister, a common response would be acknowledgement that the person referred to was not actually a real sibling. Here then is a demonstration of the power of an ideal that modern Chinese continue to uphold, one that speaks to the emotional satisfaction that arises from the feeling of kinship.

In some cases, Han Chinese and minorities have undergone parallel changes. Urban Han Chinese and Mongols in the 1980s seemed to perceive their kin networks in much the same way. Both saw their kin as inclusive of both the paternal and maternal relatives. But geographic mobility, which has accompanied the newfound prosperity of many urbanites, has resulted in less frequent visits to kin in other households. This makes it easy to forget one's connection to uncles and aunts, to say nothing of distant cousins. However, grandparents on both sides of the family seem to hold a special place, even in these newly prosperous urban households. Informants reliably recall their grandparents from either side of the family, and often, without any prompting, describe warm relationships with one or more grandparents. A twenty-two-year-old Hohhotian noted that she had lived with her grandmother for the first two years of her life, but that she "had lunch with my [paternal] grandmother once middle school started, every day for the next ten years." She added, "I feel so close and warm being around her." In this way, what was once a formally organized and somewhat restricted patrilineal descent group has been transformed by the emergence of bonds that are almost entirely based on positive emotional experiences.

PROXIMITY, FRIENDSHIP, AND RELATEDNESS

Stafford found that in certain north Chinese villages, kinship mainly comprises social bonds whose primary feature is the feeling of connectedness experienced by the individuals at their center (Stafford 2000). There are two ways in which this emotional development is manifest: interaction can be organized around a system of mutual obligations between parents and children that involves the transfer of money and the sharing of food, or a set of calculated relationships may intentionally be "constructed between friends, neighbors and acquaintances" (Stafford 2000:38). These forms of relatedness differ in their level of emotional involvement and in the degree of ethical obligation they entail. The more intimate encounters are reserved for some members (usually the mother or a same sex sibling) of the natal family and the occasional close friend, whereas a more reserved psychological posture is extended to neighbors and acquaintances. Stafford also finds a significant variation based on gender. Women are often better than men at manipulating tacit rules or problematic situations to their own benefit. Women in these contexts can't be seen as trapped within a male-centered formal kinship system, but rather as in a position to pursue distinct strategies that may be uniquely beneficial to them (Santos 2006:329). Margery Wolf (1972) was one of the first researchers to call attention to a distinctive female strategy based on what she labeled the uterine family. According to her, females skillfully worked to build strong emotional bonds with their children. Such bonds often proved very useful as her children grew up and her bonds with them offered her protection from a husband or mother-in-law who might turn hostile or combative. Wolf's insight was significant not only in that it offered a new understanding of female strategies but also because it encouraged a focus on the way real family members relate to each other in practice rather than on the more abstract notions about kinship structures typical of previous work. To this end, the Chinese family is best seen as a corporate organization, but one that is actually alive with personal and emotional dimensions.

Adopting a "practice" approach to the study of kinship, Goncalo dos Santos (2008:353) focused on the way kinship bonds are established and practiced in a southern Chinese village. He discovered that in South China, throughout the late Imperial era, it was common for individuals born in the same year but who were not related biologically or through marriage, to refer to each other as brother or sister. Dos Santos sees this type of relatedness as a special form of friendship that is conceptualized as belonging more to the kinship or family sphere rather than being perceived as an independent category with no kinship-like features. Friends of this type are somewhat equivalent to being family members rather than outsiders. The "same year sibling" relationship differs from other "sworn brotherhood" bonds in that it begins in childhood, is based on egalitarian relations, and is organized around feelings of affection. In contrast, sworn brotherhood relationships are formed in adulthood and are based on explicit goals of economic and social benefit through mutual aid. Moreover, sworn brotherhood is hierarchical, as it typically includes a leader who has a group of loyal followers (Dos Santos 2006:545, Gallin and Gallin 1997, Jordan 1985, Nye 2000).

A similar pattern can be found in urban China where individuals who are outside the formal (for instance, bilateral or patrilineal) genealogical systems are frequently transformed through affectionate feelings from casual friends into close quasi-kin through the idiom of kinship. It is conventional practice for parents to instruct their child to call a visiting acquaintance or a close friend *shushu* (uncle) or *ayi* (aunt). Further, in China's countryside but not in the city proper, it is common for children to address strangers as *shushu* or *ayi*. Susanne Brandtstader (email correspondence, 2007) observed a similar pattern in southern China where it was customary to address younger people unknown to an individual as *didi* or *meimei*. Both terms are associated with membership in a patrilineal descent system and thus attest to the lingering symbolic efficacy of that system. It is also common for friends to use fictional kin terms to refer to one another as older or younger brother (*gege/didi*), or older or younger sister (*jiejie/meimei*). For example, we often observed that when we were with a friend who happened to meet someone he knew, he would hug him and say, "He is my older brother" or "He is my younger brother." Upon learning that the ethnographer was a long-time friend they immediately said, in effect, "If you are my older brother's friend then you are my friend." In this way, close friends are transformed through equivalency into virtual members of an individual's conjugal family. It is significant that Chinese, like most people, continue to reserve their strongest bonds for their more immediate blood relatives from either side of the family. This is not a new phenomenon; Rubie Watson (1985) found a similar psychological orientation and behavioral pattern in rural southern China.

The subject of friendship has been a recurrent theme in Chinese literature. Most scholars have preferred to approach the subject of friendship through a related, albeit different, set of relationships often characterized as *guanxi* (or connections), with some scholars noting that *guanxi*'s instrumental aspect is only part of the story (Yan 1996; Yang 1994). *Guanxi* encompasses a spectrum of affective relationships that can range from straightforward exchange to more complicated personal entanglements (Smart 1999). The importance of *guanxi* relationships in daily life has declined somewhat in importance with the return of market relationships in the Reform Era. The market economy operates with a set of principles that do not require people to enter into a dependency relationship in order to conduct business—which was the case when the state dominated every aspect of the Chinese economy. For ordinary urban Chinese, the market, and the individual's access to money, has weakened the importance of government officials and administrative power generally in their lives. The shift in China's political economy has resulted in a corresponding deemphasis in ordinary conversation about the importance of *guanxi*. Coterminous with the weakening of *guanxi* in ordinary life has been an increase in the importance of friendship. Clearly what has remained vital is the value of social networks and thus communication with other people. In this way, the importance of "weak ties" between casual acquaintances (Granovetter 1973) is expanding not because of the need to obtain material things but because of the desire for vibrant personal interaction.

The establishment of a personal connection does not in and of itself produce an expectation or a sense of being related (Smart 1999). At best, it engenders a momentary feeling of solidarity. It is equivalent to the rush an individual may experience upon unexpectedly meeting someone from their native place or hometown, or discovering they share a similar hobby with someone. The connection is always a fleeting one. If a sense of relatedness develops out of an affinity of shared ideals or with frequent interaction, it will do so in one of two ways: through membership in an association or the embracing of a collective identity that serves as a basis for the construction of social borders; or through the transformation of a relationship into a special friendship usually involving a linguistic shift with the person now being referred to as "my older or younger brother or sister." Both sets of connections involve a normative ethical commitment and obligation. It is this ethical obligation that transforms a relationship from a casual association into a more personal and thus salient form of involvement.

Unlike in the early 1980s when people sought to expand their social networks out of a need to survive, today people do so to thrive psychologically. As one forty-two-year-old woman noted: "You Americans tend to be lonely a lot, but I have so many friends, not a day goes by when we do not connect in some way." For her, extensive networking devoted to the practices and process of enlarging and maintaining link-ups is an extension of her "self" and thus a confirmation of her presence in the lives of others (Jankowiak 2006:121). The shift from a *guanxi*-centered to friendship-based idiom is consistent with China's shift in its political economy. It is consistent with the shift from a unilineal-based system to a more egocentric system of relatedness. It also suggests that friendship bonds contribute to urban stability through linking individuals to one another and thus prevent, to some extent, the stresses that may stem from urban isolation.

RECONFIGURING THE MULTIGENERATIONAL FAMILY: THE DUELING GRANDPARENTS

The multigenerational family is not unique to China. It can also be found throughout Europe and North America. Until around the 1980s, it was based partly on the establishment of a strong grandfather-grandson ethical relationship. The strength of this bond could be seen in the organization of Chinese funerals for men where one or more of the deceased's grandsons wore a red ribbon as a sign that the man died with the benefit of having two generations outlive him. This was called a "red happiness," as it was a time of both grief and celebration given that the man had died knowing his line would continue. It is common for a grandfather who might have assumed a more aloof posture as a father toward his son to demonstrate public affection toward his grandson. This selective pattern of behavior is consistent with the logic of patrilineal descent, especially in traditional rural contexts. Since only males will remain in their home village and thus potentially reproduce themselves and work the farm, sons (but not daughters, who married out) were celebrated and honored as the more worthy gender. This preferential sex bias eventually changed. What has been less known and appreciated is how the structural reality of having an only child is reshaping the way maternal and paternal grandparents are relating to each other through efforts to see their only grandchild.

There is a strong interdependency between parents and grandparents on one hand and the only child of the parents on the other, a child who may well be the only grandchild of the grandparents as well. The strength of the emotional bond between alternating generations is evident in the way the parents of millennial Chinese are coming to embrace their role as grandparents. Because the patrilineal ideal is no longer critical, urban Chinese have come to live in a de facto bilateral universe organized around sentiment with ethical obligations subject to a degree of negotiation. Both paternal and maternal grandparents may seek to claim rights to access their only grandchild. In the pursuit of their interests, there has been the emergence of a new institution that has yet to receive a name. It is organized around the sharing of responsibilities toward the rearing of the grandchild, and as an emerging institution, is as yet unencumbered with any formal norms. With four grandparents and two parents focusing on a single offspring, urban Chinese must deal with negotiations over issues concerning their rights and responsibilities with respect to the child. Taken together, these negotiations are reshaping what was once a patrilineally grounded extended family into something more like a quasi-bilateral multigenerational family, one that includes both maternal and paternal lines. The bilateral multigenerational family is not, as in the case of friendship created between same-year siblings and sworn brotherhoods, an automatic formation, but rather requires a deliberate effort for the establishment of a warm and intimate bond based on mutual sentiment.

The grandparent-grandchild relationship is a significant one for some very practical reasons. For most families, the grandparents serve for a number of years as the primary provider of childcare. It is not uncommon for parents to turn over their only child to one set of grandparents who will serve as the child's caregivers for a period of time that might be only a few months but could extend until the child finishes secondary school, that is, at the age of seventeen or so. Moreover, there is often a struggle between maternal and paternal grandparents over the right to care for the grandchild. Their primary motive is likely to be the desire to establish an intergenerational emotional bond. Most urban grandparents seem anxious to nurture and feel bonded to their only grandchild.

In small rural townships or villages the primary caretaker is usually a grandparent from the father's side of the family, while in urban centers there is less emphasis on upholding patrilineal traditions in favor of flexibility. Thus, both maternal and paternal sides of the family are often actively engaged in parenting. Rural migrants who move to the city for work often leave their child (or children) behind with the paternal grandparents. The hope is that someday they can bring their children to join them in the city. Others bring their children to the city but if they cannot afford the urban school tuition, they will have to send them back to live with their paternal grandparents. In most rural areas, people continue to follow patrilineal lines of affiliation, which favor the male over the female side. This does not mean children grow up without forming bonds with their mother's side of the family; they clearly do (Watson 2007). However, it does mean that the father's side is formally favored in terms of rights and responsibilities concerning raising the grandchildren. Separating the child from the busy parent in order to allow the (most likely retired) grandparent to provide childcare has resulted in some children not adjusting well. There is evidence of depression, loneliness, and poor academic performance. This arises not due to grandparental caretaking but rather from the child forming attachment bonds with one set of kin and then being forced to break those bonds out of necessity when their parents' employment or residential situation requires it. Grandchildren are sometimes victims in China's relentlessly churning patterns of growth. In urban areas the families that appear to have the better adjusted children are the ones where everyone is actively involved in raising the child. In this context the child bonds with everyone and is abandoned by no one.

The pervasiveness of multigenerational parenting is evident in a multisite survey of 3,800 households by Susan Short and her colleagues (Short et al. 2001). This survey, conducted between 1989 and 1993 in eight provinces and autonomous regions, found that one-third of the children experienced some form of multigenerational parenting. In our Hohhot survey conducted in 2000, we found that 213 out of 261 (82 percent) of the people interviewed had lived for a time with a grandparent. There was little evidence of a patrilateral bias. For example, 111 out of 261 (45 percent) respondents lived for a period of time with their paternal grandparents, while 102 out of 261 (39 percent) lived with their maternal grandparents. Forty-eight respondents did not live with grandparents on either side. The average length of time living with a grandparent ranged from one to sixteen years, with the average length being 8.16 years. The length of time spent with a grandparent, however, does not tell the entire story. When asked which grandparent a singleton feels closest to, the majority indicated that it was their mother's mother.

The emerging Chinese multigenerational family is a fragile institution. The relationship between the paternal and maternal grandparents is seldom close. There is, therefore, an uneasy alliance between all interested parties who are also potential rivals in their efforts to gain greater access to the scarce resource that is their only grandchild. The arena in which most negotiations take place is often their adult offspring's home. If one set of grandparents is perceived as being unreasonable, the other set will appeal to their offspring (whether son or daughter) for support. This results, more often than not, in the mother's side being favored. The pattern is consistent with earlier studies conducted in the US and in Germany (Buss 2008). The sum of these interactions and transactions constitutes the essence of what we consider Hohhot's newest institution: the dual multigenerational family.

The Chinese data here stands in contradiction to William Goode's (1963) conjugal loyalty thesis, which claims there is a close relationship between the level of urbanization and the degree of conjugal intimacy: the greater the urbanization, the less inclined the couple is to defer to its elders. However, the fact that European and Chinese grandparents devote a great deal of time and effort to establishing ties with their grandchildren (Attias-Donfut and Segalen 2002:284) reveals the continuing value of intergenerational connections. The extensive involvement of Chinese grandparents with their grandchildren is also consistent with more recent studies of kinship and family interaction in the US (Lawton et al. 1994).

Although the dual multigenerational family is common in other parts of the world, it had no official existence in traditional Chinese society where the patrilineal descent system legally and definitively elevated the rights of the father's kin over the mother's. In this milieu, intergenerational ties were primarily unilineal (Watson 1985). All this changed under socialist China's policies that were designed to create a new, more egalitarian society. The party's expectation and policies that required younger women to work made childcare, especially infant care, a pressing concern. As in many eastern European countries (such as the Czech Republic and Hungary), grandparents from either side of the family stepped into the void and performed the necessary childcare. In time, the extensive involvement of grandparents with their grandchildren established a stronger, more vibrant relationship. In urban China this pragmatic adaptation undermined the principle of patrilineal descent as it was imagined and practiced in traditional times.

Chinese grandparents believe in staying connected to their roots. For most, caring for a grandchild provides a sense of fulfillment and is seldom regarded as onerous. When asked what a sixty-six-year-old grandmother got from spending so much time with her granddaughter, she replied, "I enjoy taking care of her." Another sixty-four-year-old grandmother simply said, "She is me." This point was echoed by a seventy-two-year-old grandfather who declared, while hugging his three-year-old grandson, "He is my life." A grandparent's involvement does not depend on the sex of the grandchild. We found no evidence of a sex bias: a granddaughter was embraced just as readily as a grandson.

It is the grandparents' involvement in the rearing of their grandchildren that has reshaped many urban Chinese families into a blend of conjugal loyalties and bilateral, multigenerational, emotional linkages. But the new patterns of childcare may undermine the affective bonds a child feels toward his or her parents, especially toward the mother. For example, a thirty-four-year-old woman confided: "I feel more comfortable with my grandmother than I do with my mother. I did not listen to her [i.e., her grandmother] as I know what she had to tell me about the contemporary world was nonsense. Her ideas were old. But

I simply enjoyed being around her." Another twenty-nine-year-old woman said, "My mother [who did not raise her] is always ordering me to do this or that. She makes lists. I still resist her. We are NOT close." However, she added: "This is not the case when I am with my grandmother. I just want to sit next to her."

CONCLUSION

The social transformation of the Chinese family is intertwined with a reconfiguration of parenting styles. The bonds characteristic of the emerging multigenerational family, in conjunction with the friendships that are established in school and workplace, are superseding the obligations that, in the Maoist era, were closely tied to the neighborhood, the work unit, and other formal, government-sponsored organizations. In areas that have not yet been profoundly affected by urban development, neighbors' sense of relatedness continues to mirror those typically found in the Maoist era, but in more cosmopolitan settings, physical proximity as a basis for the establishment of close relations has completely disappeared. Relatedness based in a shared ethnicity remains vibrant in multiethnic cities, for example among the Mongols and the Hui of Hohhot. Finally, bonds between parents and children remain strong with emotional involvement and obligations flowing both ways. Although a remnant of a patrilineal descent ideology continues to be a force in many symbolic arrangements characteristic of ritual events (such as funerals and marriages), it has lost much of its significance and power to organize an individual's life strategies, at least in China's cities. This is especially true for China's singleton generation, in which the old patrilineal ideology is significantly weakened and, in many instances, even nonexistent.

In urban settings, maternal and paternal interests are creating a complex and somewhat fluid family system. The conjugal family is the primary family unit, but its monopoly over a child's affection is diluted by the continuing involvement of the grandparental generation. The dual multigenerational family now serves as a primary reference for the construction of kinship obligations. The persistence with which grandparents participate in what has become essentially an intergenerational enterprise dedicated to raising their only grandchild is a key to our understanding of the contemporary Chinese family, urban society, and the human condition generally.

3 | Chinese Families: Ethnic Variations

Xinjiang Uyghurs

Uyghurs uphold the highest level of morality and filial piety. My daughters behave, never wear makeup in front of me and never speak loudly at home. They have good table manners. My sons respect me very much and never smoke in front of me.

> (A sixty-nine-year-old retired worker, from Xiaowei Zang's unpublished field notes)

Tibetans

For Tibetan brothers, the question is whether to trade off the greater personal freedom inherent in monogamy for the real or potential economic security, affluence, and social prestige associated with life in a larger, labor-rich, polyandrous family.

> (Goldstein 1987:44)

Mosuo

[Dongbao Xibi] was older than I and had treated me as a kid. This time around, he saw that I had grown into a young woman. He spent a lot of time playing with me. He asked me: "Can I stay overnight at your house?" I felt very excited. Without knowing what to say, I just nodded in consent. Late that night, Dongbao Xibi came to my room to stay with me. At that time, my mother had already gone to sleep and my brothers had gone out to visit their *axiao* (lovers).

(Shih 2010:86, reprinted by permission of Stanford University Press)

We can't escape the fact that in both ideal and practice, "the family" in China today is characterized by diversity at least as much as it is by any tendency toward a standard type. This is true because of regional traditions that distinguish the Cantonese speakers of the deep south from the Shanghainese speakers of the Yangzi River delta, for example, and both of these from those Beijing natives whose families have spoken a version of Mandarin for generations. There are, in fact, countless varieties of the Chinese language whose distinct, local qualities tend to distinguish, as do other ethnic markers such as food preferences, one Chinese region from another. This variation can also be seen in the diversity of family forms typical of China.

Beyond this are the distinctions that competing political regimes have brought to different Chinese areas. The island of Taiwan has, since 1949, been the home base of the Republic of China, a polity that traces its roots back to the days before 1949 when it ruled mainland China from the city of Nanjing. The Great Proletarian Cultural Revolution and other mass movements initiated by the Chinese Communist Party on the mainland did not directly affect Taiwan's Chinese families, simply because the non-Communist Nationalist Party controlled Taiwan. Similarly, the former British Crown Colony of Hong Kong was under British authority from the nineteenth century until its return to mainland China in 1997. Its sociopolitical experience means that the Chinese families living there confronted experiences entirely different from those faced by the people living directly under the authority of the Chinese Communist Party. Even today the people of Hong Kong live under a separate regime and this "separate system" makes their experiences different from those of mainland families.

But by far the greatest variation in family form is that found in non-Han minority groups. The PRC government officially recognizes fifty-five such minority "nationalities," and here we can only consider a few of these. The one thing they have in common is that, though their members are Chinese citizens, they are not "Han" Chinese. The Han

Chinese are those who speak Mandarin or some other version of Chinese as their first language, and who identify with the Chinese literary tradition and with the great Chinese dynasties of the past, such as the Han and the Tang. They make up over 90 percent of China's population, but they have, until they expanded under recent migrations to the north and west, occupied a relatively limited portion of China's territory. Though the Chinese state has been mainly controlled by the Han majority (though not, it should be said, during the Manchu dominated Qing dynasty), about half of the territory now considered part of the PRC has long been occupied by non-Han ethnic minorities. Some of these territories are administered at the provincial level as "autonomous regions." The word "autonomous" implies that the minorities that had traditionally occupied these areas now govern themselves with some degree of autonomy. In practice, however, the political autonomy of these regions is quite limited and China's Han-dominated central government continues to control them closely.

Province-level regions include the following:

The Tibet Autonomous Region
The Xinjiang Uyghur Autonomous Region
The Inner Mongolia Autonomous Region
The Ningxia Hui Autonomous Region
The Guangxi Zhuang Autonomous Region

These regions taken together include a large swath of territory stretching from Tibet and Xinjiang on China's extreme west and northwest, across its northern borderlands to the extreme northeast, where China shares a boundary with Russian Siberia. The provinces of Yunnan and Sichuan in southwestern China are also home to a diverse cluster of minority peoples. And, finally, the Zhuang, China's largest minority in terms of population, live mainly in the Guangxi Zhuang Autonomous Region just north of the Vietnamese border.

Though these minority ethnic groups or nationalities occupy a large percentage of China's territory, they have had a limited impact on PRC policies. This is mainly because their populations are relatively small, making up only about 8 percent of China's total population.

A great deal has been written about China's minorities, though most of this writing has been focused on ethnic and national identity. No doubt this focus is driven partly by the Chinese government's somewhat arbitrary division of minority populations into fifty-five official ethnic entities. More than a few minority communities believe they were miscategorized in the government's official system, and among these are the Mosuo, to be discussed further below. Despite the widely available writings on ethnic identity among China's minorities, other aspects of minority lives, such as family and kinship systems, are less well known. One exception to this lack of data on minority families is Yan Ruxian's 1986 compendium, *Zhongguo shaoshuminzu hunyin jiating*. This Chinese-language source offers a rudimentary overview of marriage customs and family norms among China's fifty-five ethnic minorities organized by geographic region. This is one of the few summaries on this topic. Regrettably for English speakers it is as yet only available in the original Mandarin.

Southwestern China, particularly Yunnan and Guizhou Provinces and the Guangxi Zhuang Autonomous Region, are notable for the great variety of minority groups that are native to them. The Guangxi Zhuang Autonomous Region is even officially identified in its name with the Zhuang minority that makes up about one-third of its total population. In fact, most of the studies on minority marriage are taken from cultures in southwestern China, where so many minorities reside. A notable example of such studies is Shanshan Du's *Chopsticks Only Work in Pairs: Gender Unity and Gender Equality Among the Lahu of Southwest China*. Du focuses on the private lives of the Lahu, with a particular emphasis on understanding their emotional world. In Lahu communities, gender roles are organized less in accordance with a complementary division of labor and more according to a pronounced expectation of sharing, or gender-role equality, whereby men and women do almost everything together. This remarkable study shows that emotional intimacy is the psychological glue that holds the conjugal bond together. It provides valuable insights on the topics of gender and the power of conjugal intimacy that have implications reaching beyond the lives of the Lahu. In some ways, Du's description of Lahu conjugal intimacy brings to mind many of the same ideals and behavior patterns familiar to twenty-first-century Westerners. In other ways, of course, the Lahus' romantic and marital experiences diverge from those typical of the West.

Sara Friedman (2006), in a study of Hui'an residents in southeastern China, focuses not on marriage per se, but on female solidarity and friendship. Friedman's ethnography is unique in that it describes a community that is Han in most regards, but that maintains customs native to coastal regions of south China and that seem to predate the Sinification of this area (see Stockard [1989] for an account of another south Chinese area where marital residence and other aspects of gender relations differ from those of most Han). Friedman explores the social practices of marriage, labor, and dress in China's postsocialist era in light of the changes brought about in response to policies initiated over the past sixty years, with special reference to the ways these policies have led Hui'an couples to redefine intimacy.

In northwestern China, another area with prominent non-Han populations, Xiaowei Zang (2007, 2012) has investigated Hui and Uyghur minorities, comparing them with Han Chinese in light of gender ideals, family, and society. His quantitative study of the northwestern city of Lanzhou compares ethnicity to social class as factors that shape the lives of the Hui (2013). Zang has also published work on Uyghur women with a focus on religiosity, gender inequality, and the sexual division of labor in the household. Dautcher, also focusing on a Uyghur community in Xinjiang, considers gender relations with particular attention to evolving ideas of what it means to be masculine. As will be discussed further below, he notes some features of gender relations among the Uyghur that are not typical of Han Chinese.

Of China's many ethnic minorities, we will outline here three in particular: the Uyghurs, the Tibetans, and the Mosuo. The Uyghurs and Tibetans are well worth considering in any discussion of China, given that they occupy large sections of western and northwestern China, regions that have, during various periods in the past, been beyond the reach of the Chinese central government. Perhaps it is because of these periods of independence that elements in both of these ethnic groups have resisted the authority of the PRC government in recent decades. Their prominence, both domestically within China and, to some extent, on the world stage is undeniable. Furthermore, in the case of the Tibetans, their traditional family system is unique, and so dramatically different from that of the Han Chinese that it offers a fascinating contrast from what most observers think of as "the Chinese family." The Uyghur, on the other hand, being patriarchal and patrilineal, display similarities to the Han Chinese family system, though they are not without their own local variations.

The third ethnic minority we will discuss in some detail is the Mosuo. Like the Tibetans (to whom they are linguistically and ethnically related), they have a family system that is strikingly different from that of the Han. In fact, the Mosuo family system is famous in the annals of social science by virtue of its unique family system, a system that manages to survive and even flourish while largely forswearing marriage.

THE UYGHURS OF XINJIANG

The Uyghurs are a Turkic people whose native dialects are related to those spoken in Turkey as well as to the languages of many of the Central Asian "-stans" including, for example, Kazakhstan, Uzbekistan, and Kyrgyzstan. The Uyghur homeland, the Xinjiang Uyghur Autonomous Region, has long played an important role in China's history given that through it ran much of the eastern end of the Silk Road. The Uyghur peoples who have occupied the Silk Road oases in this region for many centuries have gradually accepted Islam as their religion, though there was a period when many of them were Buddhist.

The scattered oases of Xinjiang supported communities that married endogamously and, partly because of this, these communities often developed strong local identities. These oasis-based local identities have hindered the efforts of some Uyghur political leaders to promote a province-wide "Uyghur identity" capable of subsuming local loyalties. The central government of the PRC has looked with suspicion on the promotion of a pan-Uyghur identity, seeing it as a potential threat to the authority of the Beijing government. The ongoing struggle between Uyghur self-determination and Beijing's suspicion toward loyalties beyond its control has resulted in both heavy-handed tactics by the government and occasional acts of terrorism by some of the more militant Uyghur elements. Some Uyghurs even left China in order to fight on behalf of Islamist movements in Afghanistan and the Middle East, apparently motivated by their commitment to a pan-Islamic struggle. Even those Uyghurs who do not take a militant stand against Beijing's policies are likely to view with resentment such government policies as the encouraging of Han Chinese to settle in Xinjiang in numbers that will eventually make the Han outnumber the Uyghurs.

Though the relations between some Uyghurs and the central government of Beijing has been fraught, local policies have had few effects on family life. This is partly because traditional Uyghur families were patriarchal, patrilineal, and virilocal, and in these regards they resembled Han Chinese families. Another factor is the lack of intermarriage between Han and Uyghur (Rudelson and Jankowiak 2004). It has recently been reported that at least one county government in Xinjiang is encouraging intermarriage between Han and non-Han minorities by offering cash incentives to those who choose interethnic marriages. Cherchen County, where this policy is in place, is predominantly Uyghur, which suggests that the government's aim is to encourage Han-Uyghur marriages. Most likely this local edict is a response to President Xi Jinping's call for new policies in Xinjiang that will encourage the integration of Uyghurs into China's mainstream society (Wong 2014).

There are a number of cultural patterns through which Uyghurs symbolize their ethnic distinctness from the Han including, for example, clothing, language, religious ritual, and diet. Food is a particularly salient symbol of ethnic distinction, since Uyghurs are reluctant to eat in restaurants where Han people eat, because pork is a common element in the Han diet and Muslims in China try to avoid food from kitchens where pork has been prepared. Today Uyghur marriages are based on the free choice of the principals, as are those of the Han, but Uyghur weddings are distinctly different. The features they have in common with the Han are the transfer of the bride from her home to her new husband's household, and her inclusion into his family. Also, the elaborate ceremonial banquet offers a focal point of both Han and Uyghur weddings, but beyond these commonalities are a number of differences.

In the Uyghur neighborhood in the city of Yining, Xinjiang, described by Dautcher (2009), marriages typically involve the services of a matchmaker. A Uyghur matchmaker is likely to be an older male—not a female, which is the more common pattern among the Han. The couple ordinarily decide on their own initiative to get married, since current restrictions on male-female interactions are not such as to prevent adolescents and young adults from getting to know each other. Still, 29 percent of Uyghur marriages are arranged, according to Zang (2012). In those cases where bride and groom choose each other independently, the services of a matchmaker are nevertheless useful for deciding on appropriate gifts to be exchanged between their two families.

Among Yining's Uyghurs, a few days before the wedding day, the boy's family will host a tea for him and his friends, while a "white tea" is hosted by the girl's family on the day before the wedding itself, and to this both bride's and groom's family members are invited. The ceremony, which typically lasts three days, includes a banquet on the first day, hosted by the groom's family, to which both the bride's and the groom's relatives are also invited. Each of the following days also includes a series of banquets, the first being focused on the groom's family and the third and final one on the bride's. Women arrive early to these events, generally around noon, while the men arrive in the evening, just before the main meal is served. Males and females sit at separate tables, and the females usually leave early in the evening. This gender segregation is a feature of Uyghur gatherings that is not typical among urban Han Chinese.

A key part of the wedding ceremony occurs on the first day: the ritual declaration, thrice repeated, by the groom and the bride of their intention to wed each other. Another ritual proclamation is made by a member of the bride's family who pronounces the traditional sentence, "The flesh is yours, but the bones are ours," which is thought to alert the groom and his family that there is a limit to what they can do with regard to the bride.

It is possible for young people to legally marry without a wedding ceremony, though this is looked down on and does not usually occur except among those too poor to host the appropriate banquets. In such a case there is no formalizing of the relationship between the bride's and the groom's families, and one or both sides may feel resentment toward the other about the ad hoc way in which the marriage took place. If there are lingering bad feelings between the two families, these are sometimes alleviated by the offering of gifts after the fact (Dautcher 2009).

The patrilineal and patriarchal patterns of Uyghur families include Uyghur children inheriting their surnames from their fathers, and, depending upon the family, accepting the idea that they are members of their fathers' rather than their mothers' families. In other cases, children take their father's surname but identify with both parents.

Uyghur families continue to exhibit a strong gender segregation. Women have their areas in the household and men have theirs and, particularly when visitors are present, there is little communication between the two. However, when they are alone there can be and often is rich exchange of thoughts and feelings. Zang (2012:100) found that in Urumchi, Uyghur couples are relatively egalitarian in their interaction. Urumchi families, much like those of urbanized Han, engage in a complementary sexual division of labor whereby the women are responsible for domestic chores (e.g., shopping, cleaning, childcare, caring for elderly, and so forth). Zang (2012:103) also found that Urumchi families (again, like urban Han) engage in a complementary sexual division of labor in which the women do domestic chores, while men purchase family appliances and personal clothing. Uyghur women are responsible for most household chores including shopping, meal preparation, laundry, ironing, house cleaning, childcare, and elderly care (Zang 2012:99).

The complementary division of labor often results in each sex holding exaggerated stereotypes about the other sex's domestic abilities. For example, a forty-five-year-old Uyghur male university lecturer noted:

> There is no way to dismiss the father as the household head. But they do not spend much time at home. They exercise leadership by giving general ideas to their wives. Wives make tremendous contributions to their families, running the household and taking care of children. They earn respect from family members and society. They are called virtuous wives and good mothers (Zang 2012:129).

In contrast, a forty-something Uyghur woman stressed male innate incompetence to do domestic chores properly without female supervision.

Uyghur men engage in a number of behaviors that are designed to show their dominance over their wives, often including the husband verbally assaulting his wife. Though this is more tempestuous than the atmosphere found in urban Han families, it would be incorrect to infer that urban Uyghur families are thoroughly male dominated. Zang (2012) argues that the impact of urbanization, and with it female education, makes gender relations variable from household to household. When Uyghur women have access to education, including sometimes university-level education and therefore decent jobs, their marriage and family life is likely to be more egalitarian. In such a family setting, it is difficult to determine which is the dominant gender. However, when the wife has not had access to education and has had numerous children to care for, there is a clear division of influence with the husband assuming a more controlling role. All in all, urban Uyghur family organization is shaped not so much by traditional Islamic ideology as by the limitations of educational and employment opportunities available to some Uyghur women. In sum, the patrilineal, patriarchal, and virilocal standards by which Uyghur families are organized make them similar in many ways to those of the Han. There are, however, some cultural patterns that distinguish them, particularly in the tenor of male-female, and hence, husband-wife, relationships. These differences too, are subject to change as China's prosperity grows and its trend toward urbanization continues.

THE POLYANDROUS TIBETANS

Where the Uyghurs are characterized by family systems that are similar to those of the Han, the Tibetans embrace family systems that operate according to entirely different cultural blueprints. Tibetans have traditionally occupied a great deal of territory beyond Tibet itself.

Historically Tibetans have, of course, predominated in the Tibet Autonomous Region (TAR or, simply, Tibet) but also in the province of Qinghai just to the north of the Tibetan plateau. Furthermore, parts of the neighboring provinces of Yunnan, Sichuan, Xinjiang, and Gansu also include large Tibetan communities, as do some of those areas in India, Pakistan, and Nepal that lie just over the border from Tibet.

A number of Tibetans are pastoral, subsisting on herds of yak and sheep, while others combine animal herding and agriculture. Typically, in these mixed subsistence groups, some male family members stay behind to tend the agricultural land while others accompany the animals as they move from place to place in search of good pasture. In addition to these nomadic and semi-nomadic Tibetans are those sedentary communities that depend on agriculture, trade, or urban employment.

Tibet has long been a source of political trouble for the People's Republic of China. Certainly most Tibetans would have preferred to be left alone rather than subjected to Beijing's strict, Marxist-inspired authority of the 1950s and subsequent decades. Actually some of the sources of tension between Tibetans and the PRC government stem from the profound differences in culture between Han Chinese and Tibetans, and some of the more important of these differences are specifically matters of family structure.

Given Chinese official sensibilities about Tibet, particularly after a major Tibetan uprising in 1959, travel and research in this area has been very limited until recently. Consequently, a number of research projects on the Tibetan family are based either on Tibetan refugees in Nepal or India, or on long-established Tibetan communities in those countries. Currently restrictions are loosening up to some extent, so new information about Tibetan families in Tibet proper is now starting to become available.

Traditional, pre-1950 Tibetan families followed cultural prescriptions that allowed for more variation than were typical of the Han in late imperial China (Tien 1988). The traditional Tibetan kinship system reflected a patrilineal bias in that, for example, inheritance of property was mainly through males, as was family membership. However, there were thought to be significant kinship connections through females as well. The concepts of "bone" and "blood" respectively expressed patrilineal and matrilineal connections. Many of these traditional features of the Tibetan family still prevail today.

The traditional Han Chinese family ideology, compared to that of the Tibetans, was more explicitly skewed in favor of male power. For the Han Chinese, in almost all cases, property was inherited through males, residence was virilocal, and ancestor worship was focused on patrilineal forebears. Finally, control over female sexuality was extreme, both for unmarried and married women. There was a Han ideal image of female sexual purity according to which a woman who had had extramarital sexual relations should, in order to redeem her virtue, commit suicide, even in cases of rape (Tien 1988). In Qing dynasty China and in the early twentieth century, female sexual "purity" was an issue not to be taken lightly. There were, of course, courtesans and other sex workers who did not adhere to these prescriptions against extramarital sex, but they comprised a small minority of Han Chinese females, and their reputations were stigmatized because of their unrestricted sexuality.

Though Tibetan culture did not emphasize male superiority to the extent that traditional China did, there were, nevertheless, some long-standing indications of male bias in Tibet. Patrilineal inheritance, along with relatively small dowries, meant that females' control over property was limited compared to that of males. And Childs notes that common names for daughters were "Three Is Enough," "Four Is Enough," and so on, these names being given to third and higher-order daughters with the hope that future births would produce only males (Childs 2003:439). Furthermore, most marriages entailed the transfer of the bride from her natal family to that of her husband on the wedding day. According to Fjeld (2005), members of the nobility led the bride to her new home on a pregnant horse, while commoner brides were led, on foot, by a few of their male kin.

One indication of the disadvantaged position of Tibetan women comes from Levine's 1988 study of the Tibetan Nyinba of Nepal. Here the statuses of slaves and of females were seen as overlapping where household work was concerned. Labor that ordinarily fell to women—food preparation and much of the agricultural work—could be done not only by women but by slaves of both genders. Though slavery and serfdom were abolished by the Chinese, some effects of these traditional institutions continue to influence Tibetan families in China and elsewhere (Levine 1988; Goldstein 1971; Fjeld 2005).

The most striking difference between China's Confucian-based family and the traditional Tibetan family is in the preference in the latter for fraternal polyandry—a marriage system in which two or more brothers share a single wife. The idea of two or more men sharing a wife was viewed as deeply inappropriate in China proper, though, as Sommer (2015) has shown, during the Qing dynasty, destitute Chinese families sometimes resorted to practices that amounted to men sharing a wife, a kind of de facto polyandry. Polyandry was not a low-status practice in Tibet, however, where the ideal family comprised groups of brothers and their shared wife. A Tibetan wife in a polyandrous family would maintain the household for her husbands and be sexually available to all of them, at least all of them who were of age. Polyandry and multiple marriage in general have been outlawed in China since 1950, but polyandry continues to flourish today in Tibetan cultural areas outside of the PRC, and is making a comeback in some rural areas of Tibet proper, Chinese law notwithstanding (Fjeld 2005; Goldstein, personal communication).

Fraternal polyandry is valued because it is regarded as the best marital form by which a patrilineally inheritable estate can be kept intact across generations. In a household organized in terms of this principle, a wife will ideally sleep with all her husbands in accordance with whatever schedule or arrangement the family works out, and will show no favoritism to any of them. This, of course, can prove difficult in some cases, individual personalities being what they are.

The wife in a polyandrous household was expected to reproduce the children, particularly the sons, who would secure the family's continued existence into the next generation. She was also expected to take care of those household tasks thought of as appropriate for females: child care, food preparation and most of the agricultural work, but not plowing and sowing. The ideal family was one with an estate productive enough to support a large, multigeneration family, and in which the brothers cooperated economically, often by diversifying economic activities. It was necessary for some men to absent themselves from the household in order to follow their herds if they were pastoral or to travel to distant markets if they were involved in trade; this helped justify the Tibetan idea that the best way to maintain a family estate was through a group of closely cooperating brothers, each of whom specialized in his own economic pursuits.

Since many polyandrous families had diverse economic interests, it often happened that only one or two of a group of brothers would be home at a time, which lessened the potential competition over access to the common wife. Furthermore, there was a cultural element that helped dampen the effects of sexual jealousy, though not always with complete success: this is the deeply ingrained ideal of fraternal solidarity. Commitment to and support for one's brothers is one of the most powerful cultural precepts shaping Tibetan social relations and this value alone goes a long way toward discouraging conflict over relationships with a family's wife. Consequently, though reports of sexual jealousy among brothers were not unheard of, they were not so common or so intense as to bring about the break-up of most families where fraternal polyandry was practiced.

Attitudes toward the sexual behavior of women in Tibet has generally been less restrictive than was typical of Han China, and given this, discreet dalliances outside of marriage were often tolerated, as was premarital sex. In fact, 57.7 percent of the women in Kyirong, a district in the Tibetan Autonomous Region studied by Childs, never married, though many of them had children whom they raised as their own. Using the tax records of 1958 from Kyirong district, supplemented by interviews with about 180 of Kyirong's former residents living as refugees in Nepal or India, Childs determined that most unmarried women gave birth to illegitimate children, though their birth rate was much lower than that of married women. Married Tibetans from Kyirong had an average of about six children each, while those never married gave birth to an average of about two children (Childs 2003). Goldstein found that among the Tibetans in the Limi district of Nepal in 1975, about half of the unmarried women had children. But the average reproductive rate of unmarried women was well below that of married women, being .7 per female for the former vs. 3.3 per female among the latter (Goldstein 1987).

Since Tibetan women, like their Han counterparts, normally married according to their birth order, younger sisters were more likely than older ones to remain unmarried. If an unmarried woman was living in a household in which her brothers took in a wife, she would ordinarily, at the time of the marriage, move out of the house and into a small adjunct house of her own elsewhere on the family estate. It was thought that her presence along with the new wife of her brothers might engender conflict were she to remain in the big household. Living in her small house on the family estate, she might remain alone or take in a poor man but without the formality of marrying him. In either case, children born to this unmarried woman would not have access to heritable property, and would therefore be at an economic disadvantage when they reached adulthood. If a couple remained together as their children grew up, they would come to be regarded as legitimate, though still without any rights of inheritance. Those women who did not form a stable cohabiting relationship would also typically have children through their relationships with local men.

In families with no sons, it was not unusual for a man to marry into a family uxorilocally. Any children born to such a marriage would be considered heirs of the wife's family.

A factor facilitating polyandry was the relatively low ratio of women to men in some Tibetan communities. Among the Tibetan Nyinba of Nepal, Levine reports that the female-male ratio is about 118 males per 100 females, as opposed to the ratio of about 95 to 102 males per 100 females in most national populations. She explains this discrepancy in terms of the Tibetans' favoritism for male children and consequently for more care being given to male infants, which may result in higher female mortality (1988:74).

Almost all polyandrous Tibetan marriages were fraternal. The forms of polyandry found in such societies as that of the Nayar of south India, where the men sharing a wife were unrelated, are virtually unheard of in the Tibetan culture area. This is a reflection of the value that Tibetans place on fraternal solidarity and of inheritance practices whereby an estate is handed down from father to son, or, from fathers to sons.

Maintaining a substantial resource base is the main reason Tibetans give for their preference for polyandrous marriages. Every son in a traditional Tibetan household had a right to an equal share of the family estate. He could, if he chose, leave the family, taking the rights to his share with him and thereby begin the partitioning of the family's common property. This was a prospect that prosperous Tibetan families sought to avoid, and polyandrous marriages were helpful in preventing it. When a group of brothers took a common wife, the family property—herds or agricultural land—would not be divided into separated inheritable units. Since the resources stayed together across generations in this way, the family was able to sustain itself indefinitely at a constant level of relative prosperity.

The partitioning of a family estate not only clashed with the value of fraternal solidarity, it could threaten a household with impoverishment. If, say, a group of three brothers with their wife, their parents, and children owned land and animals sufficient to maintain everyone comfortably, then, were one brother to move out, marrying monogamously to do so, this might result in that brother having just barely enough property to get by. If he had been fulfilling a key function in the family—say, if he were the one with the connections in distant markets that facilitated trade—his departure could be a blow to the family he left behind as well. For both economic and ideological reasons, higher-status Tibetans felt a great deal of pressure for each generation of brothers to stay together as an estate-holding family. Tibetan fraternal polyandry cannot necessarily be explained as merely a response to the desire to maintain a family estate across generations, but it did facilitate unified inheritances. And the Tibetans themselves emphasize the usefulness of fraternal polyandry as a device for maintaining family holdings intact.

Goldstein, on the basis of extensive interviews with refugees from Gyantse district of Tibet, determined that class differences were crucial in determining whether or not a family preferred polyandrous or monogamous marriage. Commoners (or "serfs" as Goldstein describes them) were divided into those of relatively high status and those of lower status. Serfs of relatively high status controlled heritable estates, which they passed down patrilineally to the next generation. These commoners, known as *tre-ba*, were obligated, as families, to pay heavy taxes to their lords. Given this relation to property and taxation, it was important to keep the estate intact, and the *tre-ba* did so mainly through fraternal polyandry. As long as the brothers stayed together, the estate would not be partitioned, and as long as they shared a wife, they were virtually guaranteed to stay together.

Goldstein collected data on sixty-two primary marriages among the *tre-ba* of one village in Gyantse district, and of these thirty-two (51 percent) were fraternally polyandrous. Twenty-four (39 percent) were monogamous, while the remaining six (10 percent) were uxorilocal, with husbands being brought into households that had no sons. All six of these uxorilocal marriages were monogamous, since each household had only one daughter, or, in one case, two daughters, the second of which left to become a Buddhist nun.

The lower-ranking commoner families of Gyantse district controlled land not as families but as individuals. Some individuals received grants from their (pre-1950) lord to use specific plots of land when they came of age, but they had no control over the land after their death; it returned to the lord. Inheritance was not an issue for these lower-ranking commoners nor for those who were entirely without access to land, and consequently they had nothing to gain by having brothers share a wife. Tibetans of this stratum married monogamously on the basis of love. Each son in this class would establish his own household as he was married off, rather than continuing as a member of a large family with access to an estate (Goldstein 1971:71). Only a very few of the marriages in this class were polyandrous, and these were undertaken by those brothers who had accumulated enough wealth to be upwardly mobile and who followed the same patterns as those typical of their higher-status neighbors. Levine notes similar behavior patterns among Nyinba freedmen who had traditionally been poor and had married monogamously, but who began to imitate the fraternal polyandry of the higher-status families when they had amassed enough property to do so. Most of the marriages of the lowest ranking Nyinba men were not only monogamous but uxorilocal (Levine 1988).

Polygynous marriages were generally looked at askance because multiple wives within a single family were thought to cause conflict over resources and consequently might lead to a breakup of the family and its property. But polygynous marriages, though uncommon, did occur. A family with more than one daughter but no sons might end up with those daughters marrying both uxorilocally and polygynously. There were also some cases in which a group of brothers with a wife brought in a second wife thus creating a polygynandrous marriage. This situation was also not common but could occur if one of the younger brothers in such a family were not happy with being married to the woman his older brother had chosen. In such cases, it was preferred that the second wife be a sister of the first in order to promote domestic harmony and avoid partitioning.

One consequence of fraternal polyandry is that the Tibetan birth rate was relatively low. Certainly three or four brothers with a single, shared wife would not be likely to reproduce at the rate equal to that of a group of brothers each of whom had married monogamously. Also contributing to the low birth rate was the relatively small number of children born to women who were not married.

The children born to the wife in a polyandrous family were thought of as brothers to each other, even though sometimes individual sons were understood to be the offspring of a specific father in the senior generation. If the family held together across generations, with none of the brothers deciding to depart with his share of the estate, it hardly mattered in economic terms which son was the offspring of which father, though it did matter insofar as Tibetan men like to be able to claim to be father to one or more sons.

China occupied Tibet in 1950, and, following an unsuccessful anti-Beijing uprising in 1959, after which the Dalai Lama fled to India with a number of his followers, the influence of the government of the People's Republic of China began to have a profound impact on the lives of Tibetans. The Chinese government outlawed slavery and serfdom, and continues to justify its heavy-handed policies in Tibet in terms of the egalitarian ideals that motivated this abolition. Also, the

Marriage Law of 1950, which prohibited arranged marriages, had an impact, particularly on those Tibetans living in urban areas where the influence of the national government is strongest. Though Tibetans were forced to accommodate to the authority of the PRC government, the effects of this authority have not eliminated traditional marriage patterns.

According to Goldstein (personal communication, 2015) since the end of the Cultural Revolution (1966–76), the central government of the PRC has backed away from efforts to control the everyday lives of individuals in Tibetan regions as well as elsewhere in China. As a consequence, polyandry and polygyny, though illegal, continue to exist as ethnic variations in certain areas. In fact, even during the Cultural Revolution, officials often allowed previously established polyandrous marriages to continue. However, economic pressures worked against polyandry in agricultural areas before 1976 because collectivization meant households did not own their own land. Since a major function of polyandry was maintaining the integrity of a household's inheritance, collectivization undermined its rationale. In nomadic areas, polyandrous marriages sometimes continued throughout the collective era by virtue of the household claiming, for official purposes, that a bride brought in for the oldest brother was exclusively his, when, in fact, she was shared in the traditional manner by all the brothers. Then, around 1980, polyandry began to reemerge on a wider scale when the communes were dismantled and households once again became proprietors of heritable land.

To some extent, traditional Tibetan marital patterns have made a comeback, given the more relaxed attitude of the Chinese government today. However, forces of change such as exposure to international media, tourism, and the effects of the government's campaigns of the past are leaving their mark, and a complete return to pre-1950 patterns is not likely for Tibet.

THE MOSUO: THE PEOPLE WHO PREFER NOT TO MARRY

In the mountains of western China, just east of Tibet, on the border between Sichuan and Yunnan provinces, live the Mosuo, a people whose family system is drastically different from that of both the Tibetans and the Han. One feature making the Mosuo different is that the majority of them do not marry at all.

The Mosuo are referred to by several different names in various sources, including, for example, Moso, Mosso, and Na. According to the official record of fifty-five ethnic minorities in the PRC, the Mosuo, in fact, are not separately listed, most of them being lumped together with the linguistically related Naxi while others, mainly on the Sichuan side of the provincial border, are categorized as Mongols (McKhann 1998). The Mosuo themselves protest this categorization, claiming that their longstanding identity as a separate ethnic group with unique characteristics justifies their claim to a separate status among the officially recognized minorities. So far, their claim has not been accepted by PRC authorities. The Mosuo live in a rather isolated mountainous area and are few in number, their total population being around 30,000 (Shih 2010).

A feature that makes the Mosuo distinct from the Han, as well as from most other Chinese ethnic groups, is their matrilineality. Han, Uyghur, and Tibetan families have traditionally been patrilineal, and, generally, all three still continue to exhibit patrilineal tendencies to varying degrees. But most Mosuo have long been, and remain today, strongly matrilineal.

Individuals are born into the descent group (*sizi*, in Naru, the Mosuo language) of their mothers, and, barring adoption or other such disruptive circumstances, remain in that kin group for their entire lives. Furthermore, the typical Mosuo household consists of adults and the children of the adult females. For example, a woman, her daughters and sons, the children of her daughters and, perhaps, the children of her daughters' daughters, might comprise a household (Shih 2010).

A multigeneration Han Chinese household would likely be composed of a married couple, the sons of that couple along with their wives (who had married in from other families), and, perhaps, the children of those second-generation sons. Han Chinese daughters typically leave their natal homes upon marriage to join their husbands' families. The Mosuo, by contrast, not only define family membership through women rather than men, but usually do not include married couples in their households at all, males and females remaining with their mothers and her siblings throughout their lives. Since most of them don't marry, neither men nor women are obligated to leave home at marriage.

Mosuo households are generally based on matrilineal patterns of inheritance. However, there is a great deal of flexibility in the ways in which such houses are organized. The basic rule seems to be that women inherit the role of *dabu*, or household head, from their mother, but this is an extremely variable rule. In fact males can serve as household heads, as long as they are willing to do so, and if the adult members of the house agree that he is the appropriate person for that role. But typically the *dabu* is a female (Shih 2010).

The duties of the *dabu* include disbursing household funds to meet individual needs, which means deciding whether specific requests for funds are justified and can be borne by the household budget. The *dabu* manages household maintenance in light of the moral authority granted by household members. A *dabu* is expected to be not only competent but impartial and selfless, and only in light of these qualities will the house accept her or his authority. Management skills are important given that the *dabu* is expected to make decisions with reference to a variety of issues including organization of religious rituals, the purchases of clothing for individual members, payments for education, and assignment of tasks to specific household members (Hsu 1998; Shih 2010).

It is not forbidden for Mosuo to marry, and some in fact do. However, the most common basis for reproduction in Mosuo society is *tisese*. *Tisese* is a custom whereby a man remains in the household in which he grew up (his mother's) and establishes nonexclusive, non-obligatory, and noncontractual visitation relationships with women in neighboring households (Shih 2010). Through these relationships, children are procreated, these children being raised mainly by their mothers and their mothers' sisters and brothers. Though fathers generally do not live with the mothers of their children, they usually do offer support and affection to their offspring (Mattison et al. 2014). Most of the effort in raising the children, however, falls to their mothers and other co-resident matrilineal kin.

In Mandarin the *tisese* relationship is referred to as *zou hun*, which translates into English as "walking marriage." Since *tisese* is not actually a form of marriage, this is a somewhat misleading term, but "walking marriage" is commonly used in English language descriptions of Mosuo culture.

The *tisese* pattern of male-female relations and the matrilineal household are complementary elements in the Mosuo family system. Each one, in some ways, facilitates and responds to the other. Matrilineal kinship systems are characteristic of various societies around the world, but the *tisese* pattern, as a norm and a preferred basis for procreation, is not. In light of its uniqueness, some attention to the details of how it functions, both psychologically and structurally, is in order.

Chuan-kang Shih offers a thorough ethnographic account of *tisese* and marital relationships among the Mosuo (or, to use his term, "Moso"). Shih emphasizes the noncontractual, nonobligatory, and nonexclusive qualities of *tisese* as features that distinguish it from marriage. These qualities refer to the fact that when a man and woman begin a *tisese* relationship, they do not formalize it in a wedding ceremony as they would a marriage; neither of them is under obligation to begin the relationship and either one may end it whenever they choose. Finally, being involved in a *tisese* relationship does not exclude an individual, male or female, from being involved in one or more other *tisese* relationships at the same time, though this somewhat laissez faire attitude toward multiple relationships is currently changing to the point where expectations of exclusiveness are becoming predominant (Blumenfield, personal communication 2015).

At the heart of the *tisese* relationship is the visitation by a man of a woman in her private bedroom during the night. Typically such a relationship begins when a couple exchanges some words during a daytime encounter by which they establish that each is interested in having a *tisese* relationship with the other. Once this understanding is reached, the man will, upon nightfall, leave his own home and make his way over to that of the woman. She will either wait for him at the household's courtyard door so that she can open it when he arrives or, through a prearrangement, he may let her know of his arrival by throwing pebbles on the roof of her bedroom, whereupon she will go down to open the door for him. The couple will spend the night together but, before the household is up, he will depart, making his way back to his own residence.

As long as each member of the couple finds the other agreeable, the man will continue his visits. He may, of course, lose interest and stop visiting, or the woman may decide he is no longer welcome as a *tisese* partner and let him know he should stop showing up at her doorstep. Neither individual has a "right," so to speak, to criticize the other for termination of a relationship, but, naturally, individuals may suffer from pangs of rejection and unrequited affection when they are told their attentions are no longer desired.

Shih offers some examples of the *tisese*-based experiences of individual Mosuo from the 1950s that he has translated into English from the Chinese-language ethnography of Yan and Song (1983). The first example describes the life of a female at middle age whom the authors ask, "Would you prefer to have many *axiao* [*tisese* partners] or just a few?"

The woman answers: "When I was young, I thought the more the better. When I grow older, however, with so many children and so much work but less energy, it would be too much to have that many *axiao*, I just hope to have a stable, long-term *axiao* to see each other and to help each other." Yan and Song conclude by saying, "These words reflect the common aspiration of the local adult women" (Yan and Song 1983, cited in Shih 2010:89).

A young man's description of his first *tisese* experience includes his asking his friend, Daba, to contact the two mothers of a woman who had caught his eye (Shamu), to inquire whether his visit would be welcome. The mothers say that they are happy for him to visit their daughter, but the issue is really up to her. When Shamu agrees that she is willing to accept a *tisese* visit from the man (whose name is Aji Pinchu), he assembles some gifts for the family and makes his way to the house one evening, accompanied by Daba. He continues the story:

My heart beat faster as we were approaching the door of her house. After all, it was the first time for me to meet an axiao, without knowing how to behave, I begged Daba to stay with me for a longer while and not let me deal with her mothers by myself. Daba told me not to worry and said that the mothers of the girl would make everything just fine. Daba and I were seen before we even entered the door. The mothers cordially called us to come in. After I entered the room, I did not see Shamu there. Her absence somewhat reduced my uneasiness. (Yan and Song, cited in Shih 2010:90)

After enjoying the food and alcohol offered by Shamu's mothers, and giving them the clothing, shoes, and other gifts he had brought for them, Aji Pinchu gradually relaxes until, finally, the mothers lead him to the bedroom of Shamu, whereupon they push him in with a shove, and walk away (ibid.).

Both the woman and the man described in these accounts go through a series of *tisese* relationships, and both of them have some rewarding experiences as well as some that are disappointing. In their younger years, their *tisese* experiences resemble somewhat the kinds of affairs that young Europeans and Americans might have during their high school and university years, with all the excitement, pleasure and sorrows that these entail. Interestingly, as Aji Pinchu's story in particular illustrates, the *tisese* relationship is often a family affair. In his case, his first relationship was not, as is usually the case, a clandestine one that eventually evolves into an open one, but rather begins in the open. In fact, his initial instinct was to approach the senior-generation women for permission to proceed rather than the woman who had actually attracted his interest.

Mosuo often emphasize the benefits of the *tisese* pattern, and undeniably it does offer a number of advantages. For one thing, individuals have the opportunity to live their lives with the family in which they grew up. Given the Mosuo cultural valuation of harmony, households seem to be, more often than not, devoid of major conflicts, so remaining with one's mother, aunts, uncles, and grandmother for a lifetime has its appeal. Furthermore, there is no such thing as divorce in families that don't marry, and there is no such thing as an illegitimate child. Children, as a rule, are recognized as belonging to their mother and her family, no matter who the father may be. Finally, where there are no marriages, there can be no bad marriages, those in which spouses trapped in an unwanted relationship struggle to find happiness in spite of their obligations to a partner whom they no longer love. Shih's ethnography is titled *Quest for Harmony*, and this title suggests that, to a large extent, Mosuo find this quest fulfilled.

Most children among the Mosuo have fathers whom they recognize, even in those cases where a woman may be involved in multiple *tisese* relationships. Of course there are cases where there is some confusion over who a child's biological father is, but this is also true where marriage predominates—among the Mosuo and in other societies as well. In any case, where paternity is in question, no great tragedy will result. Individuals are more often anxious to be seen as a father rather than reluctant—as they may be in marriage-oriented societies. And fathers, as a rule, pay attention to the welfare of their children.

According to Mattison and her colleagues (Mattison et al. 2014), most Mosuo fathers today contribute to their children's well-being either through direct paternal affection, through material contributions, or through both. A father whose relationship to particular children is recognized is typically welcomed in the household of his children, and, in fact, he may offer his services to the household, stay with his *tisese* partner for days at a time, and take his meals with her and her kinsmen. This may also be the case with men who have not yet fathered children in a household in which they have a *tisese* relationship. If he is well liked by his partner's family—and this seems to usually be the case—he may virtually join the household for days at a time, to such an extent that a casual visitor might well mistake him for one of the household members. This situation may come about as a result of a *tisese* relationship which started out with clandestine visits by a man, grew to a point where the man no longer attempted to conceal his visits, and began to show up at the woman's house in the evening when the family was awake and active. A clandestine *tisese* relationship may, in other words, evolve into an open one (Shih 2010, Mattison et al. 2014).

Though most Mosuo do not marry, a minority do. The circumstances that prompt different individuals to form the long-term, contractual relationship that comprises marriage vary, though these often include a household's need for adult members of both genders in order to ensure all tasks can be covered and the family line can be preserved. Adult males are the ones who do construction and other heavy work, while females take care of lighter household chores. And, of course, females of childbearing age are essential for continuing the family line. In light of this, some households will encourage a man who has an ongoing *tisese* relationship with one of their women to formalize the relationship through marriage and move into the household permanently. Similarly, a household might invite a woman who is a *tisese* partner of one of its male members to leave her home and join the man's family in marriage. This will be particularly likely if a household is without women of childbearing age, and thereby threatened with extinction of the family line. There is also the special case of the Mosuo chief, who has traditionally married: a reflection of his regular interactions with the wider Chinese society. Also, in those parts of Mosuo territory where the environment is particularly mountainous, the majority of adults will marry. Shih believes that this is a reaction to the difficulty of making repeated nighttime visits in this rugged terrain (Shih 2010).

A measure of resentment characterized Mosuo attitudes toward the outside world during the latter half of the twentieth century. According to Shih (2010) this negative sentiment was a defensive reaction triggered by the condescending views that early Han Chinese ethnographers held regarding their family system. Since Mosuo families are female-based and include a noncontractual and nonexclusive *tisese* pattern of male-female relationships, these ethnographers categorized the Mosuo family as a leftover remnant of a primitive family form. According to Marxist theory, outlined by Engels and based partly on the work of Lewis Henry Morgan, humanity passed through a matrilineal phase in its early stages of development. Steeped in this Marxist (or, in Shih's terminology, Morganian-Engelsian) ideology, Chinese ethnographers of the early 1950s categorized Mosuo society as a kind of living fossil, one exhibiting primitive characteristics. According to Marxist ideas about the series of stages through which human societies supposedly progress, the Mosuo were in need of a good shove to bring them up to date.

That shove came in the mid-1950s with the Chinese government's heavy-handed program of "Democratic Reform." In fact, starting in 1956 and lasting up until the end of the Great Proletarian Cultural Revolution in 1976, Mosuo society in general, and male-female relations in particular, were subject to pressure from agents of the national government whose aim was to eliminate practices they regarded as backward or immoral. At the top of the list of the practices targeted by the authorities was *tisese*.

This pressure culminated with the "One Wife, One Husband" system that from 1975 to 1976 pushed 424 couples, often through economic pressure, into marriage in Yongning district. But with the end of the Cultural Revolution and the beginning of the Reform Era, the pressure on the Mosuo to conform to Confucian or officially approved ideas of marriage relented. Particularly after the 1981 disbanding of the communes in Yongning, most of the couples forced into marriage ended their formal relationships and returned to the traditional practice of *tisese*. This return to tradition was not complete, however, in that a greater emphasis was now put on the ideal of the exclusive relationship. Consequently, *tisese* relationships today are more likely to be exclusive than was the case pre-1950, and conflicts over jealousy concerning betrayals where exclusivity was presumed or desired are more common than before (Shih 2010). For the first time, phrases implying female immorality linked to sexuality appeared, one such being the insulting claim that "That woman is land already tilled" (Shih, personal communication, 2015). But for the most part, the general pattern of the Mosuo family system continues to prevail: that is, most households are matrilineally organized, most male-female relationships only endure as long as the partners themselves want them to, and paternal contributions to a child's upbringing are real, though not, usually, as substantial as the contribution of the mother and her siblings. In some ways, the *tisese* relationship calls to mind the somewhat futuristic "pure relationships" posited by Giddens and to be described further in Chapter Four: relationships that endure only for as long as the interested partners find them fulfilling (Giddens 1992).

4 | Courtship and Marriage: Twentieth-Century Transformations

In the early 1960's you had to be careful who you selected as a possible spouse. You had to check her family's political background. You had to be sure there would not be a contradiction and you would be criticized for marrying someone of the wrong class background.

(A sixty-five-year-old man, from William Jankowiak's unpublished field notes)

I am good enough to be a housewife, I want to always follow my man and support my man, if my man is busy at work, even if I also want to be a professional woman with my own life. I still can be at home, to be housewife, if he wants this, this is not a problem for me, because in my mind, the most beautiful place for me to live is my lover's heart.

(A twenty-four-year-old college-educated woman, from William Jankowiak's unpublished field notes)

In the twentieth century, China experienced a series of tumultuous episodes that shook up existing family systems and brought about dramatic changes in patterns of courtship and marriage. Behind these changes were three conflicting cultural systems or value orientations, each of whose influence rose and fell at different times in the modern era. At the beginning of the century, the traditional, Confucian values were pre-eminent. But within the first decade of the century, and particularly after 1919, in response to ever-increasing influences from the West, a globally based liberal ideology began to undermine and transform traditional values. This ideology emphasized egalitarianism, individualism, and the idealization of romantic relationships as both normal and rewarding. Then, in 1949, when the Chinese Communist Party gained control of the mainland (but not Taiwan and Hong Kong), it immediately began to promote a Maoist value system. The Communist Party idealized egalitarianism, was hostile to individualism, and was puritanically opposed to premarital sex, and leery of self-indulgent romanticism. Finally, the Maoist period was followed around 1980 by a Reform Era in which the forces of globalization reintroduced many of the liberal values that had been pushed aside during Mao's ascendance. What had emerged by the beginning of the twenty-first century was an array of family systems where regional differences, rural-urban differences, and other factors resulted in various combinations of these values systems shaping courtship and marital behavior for different individuals.

MARRIAGE AND COURTSHIP IN THE CONFUCIAN FAMILY

China's traditional family system is often characterized as Confucian due to the influence of the social philosopher Confucius who lived in the sixth and fifth centuries BCE. Though he did not actually establish all the values with which he is commonly associated, his role in crystallizing them is such that "Confucian" can reasonably be used to describe the principles on which China's traditional family system was based. These principles include, in particular, the following:

Family lines are traced through males. That is, families are based on the principle of patrilineal descent. It was understood that women without sons should be subordinate to men, which is to say, the traditional family was patriarchal. Children ideally should honor and obey their parents, and, in general, younger people should defer to their elders. For example, to show their respect, younger siblings customarily address their elder siblings by kin terms rather than by their names. Older siblings, on the other hand, are free to address their younger siblings by either kin terms or names.

Marriages were arranged by the parents with the aim of strengthening the family as a viable economic unit. Romantic and sexual inclinations of unmarried youth were suppressed by strict gender separation and an ideology that denigrated such sentiments. This allowed parents to arrange marriages based on family interests without distractions that might arise from the romantic or sexual impulses of their offspring.

At marriage, a wife was transferred to her new husband's house. Marital residence, in other words, was virilocal. A new wife served in her new household under her mother-in-law's supervision. The primary goal of the marriage was to enable the continuing of the patrilineal family line and therefore the first duty of a new wife was to produce a son.

Throughout the twentieth century, the impact of liberal and Maoist ideologies on the traditional Confucian family system steadily undermined its power, but never eliminated its influence entirely. As this process unfolded, Chinese customs in the areas of mate selection and courtship were repeatedly reconstructed in response to ever-changing ideas about individualism, gender equality, love, sex, and other aspects of life. Broadly, we can say that marriages were overwhelmingly arranged by parents as the twentieth opened, but this system gradually gave way first to a courtship culture and, by the turn of the twenty-first century, a true, entertainment-focused dating culture. Along with these trends were others that emerged in the last decade of the twentieth century, specifically, ever more open gay and lesbian subcultures as well as a trend toward the acceptance of casual sexual encounters.

The arranged marriages that were a hallmark of the traditional family system in China were supported ideologically by the Confucian value system, but were also reinforced by the economic control that most parents exercised over their offspring's future prospects. In agricultural societies (which is what traditional China was), control over inheritable land gives the senior generation a great deal of leverage over their offspring. This leverage is somewhat reduced when young people are exposed to urban environments where economic opportunities are more varied and less inheritance-dependent than they are in the countryside. But even in urban environments, the pervasive Confucian ideology that empowered males and elders, backed up by a legal apparatus that stood ready to enforce its precepts, meant that young people generally had to defer to their parents in matters of marriage. And parents, of course, considered it only right that they should control their children's marriages, given the importance of such matters in ensuring the economic viability of the household and the continuation of the patrilineal family line. In this ethos, personal sacrifice is expected for the sake of the family's well-being. Spouses' personal feelings toward each other are comparatively unimportant when it comes to loyalty, cooperation, and harmony within the larger kinship unit. In this setting marriage is never between just two people but involves a wider set of interested actors whose behavior was strongly shaped by their views of the family's interest as a corporate entity.

When bringing a new bride into the household, a groom's parents would be concerned that she be hard-working and skilled at household chores and that she not disrupt family harmony. Her labor would add to the household's viability and her relationship with her mother-in-law determined, to a large extent, whether or not harmony would prevail in the household. Chinese lore and literature are replete with stories of mother-in-law/daughter-in-law (*popo/poxi*) tensions. There was, in fact, no way to guarantee that a new bride would be a capable worker or compliant daughter-in-law. Furthermore, if her husband turned out to be particularly taken with his new wife, his mother might feel her own power was being undermined. These were the typical concerns that dominated the thinking of the elders in the patriarchal family that a new bride was destined to join. Though there were certainly many households in which the mother-in-law/daughter-in-law relations were actually harmonious, there were also many where they were decidedly not.

Traditionally, parents of a boy would consult a matchmaker by the time he reached sixteen or seventeen years of age. In seeking a spouse for their son, they would do so with an eye to the economic welfare of the family, hoping that the incoming bride would contribute to the household labor. In particular, they would want her to endow the family with one or more sons. The birth of a son was the key to the continuation of the patrilineal line and the failure of a family to produce any sons was traditionally viewed as a tragedy. One metaphor that was sometimes used for a family without a male heir was that of a house having closed its doors. The image of a closed-up house suggested a household that was "out of business," or essentially dead and on the way to extinction.

Where daughters were concerned, parents mainly wanted to make the best match possible in that having a connection to a good family could be useful for them. Even though their daughter would be leaving the household to live with her husband (in most cases), her marriage had implications for her parents' status and their ability to call on in-laws for assistance in future matters. Furthermore, most parents were naturally concerned that their daughter be treated reasonably well in her new household.

In addition to these considerations, both the bride's family and the groom's looked to cosmological forces, usually by consulting an astrologer, to make sure there were no spiritual issues arrayed against a proposed match. The ideal arranged marriage, then, brought together two families of relatively equal wealth and status (though it was acceptable for the bride's family to be of slightly lower status than the groom's) whose astrological signs, based on their respective time and date of birth, appropriately matched. Ideally the bride and groom had never seen each other before the wedding day, the arrangement for their wedding having been made entirely by their respective parents with the assistance of a matchmaker.

Traditional Chinese families went to great lengths to keep young, unmarried men and women from mingling. Women, once they reached sexual maturity, were expected to remain within the family compound for the most part. A young woman would go to the market and other such public activities only in the company of her mother or some other appropriate chaperone. By preventing any grounds for gossip about the young woman, her parents aimed to boost her marriage potential. The less she was seen in the town or village where she lived, the safer her reputation would be.

Young men were not so strictly controlled, but parents certainly did not want their sons to become romantically involved with someone of whom they did not approve. Males were also constrained by parental pressures where romantic or sexual liaisons were concerned, though not quite as much as females were. These constraints came not only from parental restrictions but also by virtue of the lack of any contexts wherein young men and women could meet. Access to females was so restricted as to render romantic affairs all but impossible for most young men. This was not entirely true in urban areas where a man from a family of means could spend time in the company of courtesans and, in some cases, even pursue an occasional love affair in that milieu. But parents would not expect their son to marry that sort of woman and, in fact, would do everything in their power to prevent such a possibility.

The focus on the patrilineal principle in traditional China meant that the bride's transfer to her new husband's house marked both the beginning of a dramatically different life for her and membership in an entirely new family. Where in the past she had kowtowed and made ceremonial offerings to her elders and to tablets representing her patrilineal ancestors, she would now begin to focus this ritual behavior on the ancestors of her husband. Confucian tradition tells women that they face three obediences: first to the father, then to the husband, and finally, as widows, to their sons. Certainly the degree to which a woman was willing to obey any of these male figures varied greatly for different individuals, but, nevertheless, the ideal was embedded in the classics and it was universally known. Polygyny could be seen in early twentieth-century China, but such marriages were practiced only by a minority of elite men. Those men who married polygynously enjoyed thereby a degree of enhanced status. Such marriages tended to put women in a difficult situation due to co-wife competition. Polyandrous arrangements were not legal but were present in late Imperial China; they did not enhance the status of those who resorted to them. Typically they were initiated by women in order to cope with extreme poverty (Sommer 2015).

There were other ways in which women's private interests could undermine or redefine classical Confucian norms. Margery Wolf's (1972) research in rural Taiwan found that women might articulate their commitment to the patrilineal and patriarchal family, but in their behavior they were careful to observe the interests of their "uterine" family, that is, the family consisting of themselves and their children and from which husbands were excluded. In this way, Chinese women were not entirely powerless. Confucian ideology and traditional habits restricted their opportunities, but within this socially restrictive environment many women carved out a more advantageous, albeit somewhat restricted, space.

On a woman's wedding day, female subordination was traditionally emphasized by various symbols, including the windowless red sedan chair in which she would be transported to her husband's home and the translucent red veil that covered her face. Unable to see through the veil, a bride would be led from the sedan chair to the couple's bedroom upon arrival at the groom's house. Sometimes other elements also suggested the woman's problematic status. She might, for example, be faced with a flashing mirror or be required to step over a smoky fire as she walked up to the groom's family home, the smoke being viewed as a purifying agent. Soon after the bride's arrival and the lifting of her veil by her husband, both she and her new groom would be subject to a kind of ritualistic teasing (known as "the disturbance in the room") as they sat together in their new bedroom. This teasing typically included having members of the groom's family pose difficult tongue twisters that the bride was required to repeat, but which, when mispronounced, were likely to be sexually suggestive and so potentially deeply embarrassing (Freedman 1966, 1970).

At the center of traditional wedding day rituals was the bowing of both bride and groom to the spirits of heaven and earth and to the groom's ancestors. This ritual was often replaced during the Maoist era by having the couple bow to a picture of Chairman Mao. Given the broadly antireligious attitude of the Communist Party during the 1950s and 1960s, bowing to ancestors or any other spiritual entities would have been evidence of counterrevolutionary attitudes. The implication that bowing to Chairman Mao was, in some sense, a suggestion that he enjoyed divine status was not ordinarily openly discussed.

A traditional wedding day generally ended with a feast to which the groom's family and friends (but not the bride's family, or only a few members of her family) were invited. During the general feasting and drinking, the couple would walk from table to table to share toasts with the guests and, in effect, to introduce the new woman to the kinsmen and neighbors who would surround her in the future.

There are a number of variations on wedding day symbolism and ritual in traditional China, but the points least likely to vary are the movement of the bride from her natal home to her husband's home; the bowing to representatives of the spiritual realm, usually including the husband's ancestors; and the culminating feast in which the bride is introduced to the family and friends of the groom. What these actions symbolize, above all, is that the bride is making a life-changing transition from being a daughter to being a wife and daughter-in-law, and that this entails a dramatic transformation in every aspect of her life.

ADOPTING A DAUGHTER-IN-LAW AND OTHER NONSTANDARD VARIATIONS ON MARRIAGE

Along with the mainstream version of traditional marriage, involving the moving of a new bride from her natal home to her husband's household, there were a number of variations pursued by different Chinese families in the past. In many Chinese communities, the custom of minor marriage was one in which a young daughter would be moved into the household of her future husband. This transfer could take place at any time after the birth of the child, which meant she would be raised alongside her future husband throughout her childhood, relating to him more or less the way a sister might relate to a brother. The drawbacks of such a scheme are obvious, and Arthur Wolf has demonstrated that such marriages are much more likely to be unhappy and to end in divorce than are the more common or "major" marriages. A fundamental problem with these adopt-a-daughter-in-law marriages is the lack of sexual interest that the husband and wife have toward each other, given that they have been living together since childhood and acting the parts of sister and brother. Wolf argues that the suppression of sexual interest due to close association in early childhood provides confirmation of the Westermarck hypothesis. According to Westermarck, incest taboos are rooted in the innate human tendency to find sexual relations abhorrent with those whom one has lived in close association with as a child (Wolf 1995). The minor form of marriage gradually declined during the twentieth century in those areas where it was most widespread and today has entirely disappeared.

Another variation from the standard traditional arranged marriage was the uxorilocal marriage in which a new husband moved into his wife's family. Such a marriage might cause structural complications for a family. A woman was supposed to obey her father until marriage, and afterwards her husband. By remaining in her father's household after her marriage a woman would be forced to divide her loyalties or choose between parents and spouse. There were other problems with such marriages. Since continuing the patrilineal family line was such a fundamental obligation for every son, a man who abandoned his own family and moved into his wife's household was, in most cases, surrendering his offspring to his in-laws' family line. That is, the children born to him and his wife would usually take her family name and grow up worshiping her ancestors, not his own. There were cases in which a man making an uxorilocal marriage might negotiate to have some of the offspring designated as his own family's heirs, but nonetheless, his status would suffer by virtue of his having resorted to the uxorilocal form. A man would not accept such a marriage unless his situation were quite desperate by virtue of his poverty or his family having so many sons that their resources could not support the expenses entailed in standard marriages for all of them. A woman whose family brought a husband in through such a marriage was also vulnerable to criticism, since they were marrying their daughter to a low-status man. However, if a family had only daughters, this was a way to ensure a continuation of the family line, even though it was not an ideal arrangement (Wolf 1972).

Some women did not accept the patriarchal family arrangement. In south China's Canton Delta region many women tried to resist marriage altogether. Stockard (1989) has described an array of behaviors where women practiced "delayed transfer marriage" or declined to marry at all. These practices were particularly prominent in the nineteenth and early twentieth centuries and seem to have their origins in practices of non-Han minorities who occupied this region before its

Sinification. In a delayed transfer marriage, the bride would return to her natal home after her wedding and then only visit her husband on festive occasions for a few years or until she became pregnant. Such a practice violated orthodox Confucian ideas about husband-wife relations, and a number of government officials in the nineteenth century actively sought to put an end to the practice.

Conflicts arose from local customs that granted women more freedom than Confucian ideology allowed, and some wives, caught in this conflict, resorted to suicide. Others found ways to avoid living with their husbands until old age by paying "compensation" to them and thereby allowing them to bring in a second wife who could bear him children. Then the first wife, having paid for her freedom from marriage, could eventually move in with her husband's family in her old age.

Another option in this region was for a woman to perform a spirit marriage in which she would formally marry the spirit of a deceased man, thus providing herself with a lineage to which she could belong while avoiding the difficulties associated with life as a wife and daughter-in-law. Finally, some women declined to marry altogether by residing in "girls' houses" with other sworn spinsters. In such houses the ordinary rituals associated with family membership could be carried out but again, without the troubles that having in-laws might entail. What all of these unorthodox patterns had in common were a tendency to provide women with more breathing space than they might expect to find in a traditional major marriage. They were also apparently sustained by the booming silk culture of the Canton Delta area, which, up until the 1930s, provided female workers in the sericulture industry with the economic means to either buy their way out of a marriage or otherwise resist male domination.

All of these variations on the orthodox Confucian model of marriage—minor marriage, uxorilocal marriage, delayed transfer marriage, and so on—indicate that there was not a single pattern that all men and women were obligated to follow in traditional China. However, there certainly was a dominant pattern, and this was the one laid down by Confucian orthodoxy, an ideology that pointedly privileged men over women and elders over the young and that required that a bride move into her husband's house on her wedding day. The variations were either denigrated as inferior to the ideal form (such as uxorilocal marriage and minor marriage) or were local variations, not practiced in all Han Chinese regions (delayed transfer marriage).

THE ROOTS OF "FREE LOVE" AND THE END OF ARRANGED MARRIAGE IN CHINA

It was commonly assumed that the idea of love-based marriage was introduced to China as a result of contact with the West in late Imperial and early Republican times (ca. 1850–1920). But this somewhat simple narrative misses an important aspect of both romantic love and Chinese cultural traditions. It is not the case that young Chinese suddenly decided, after centuries of arranged marriage, that Westerners had a gift, the gift of love, and that this should be incorporated into Chinese society. In fact, romantic love has had a place in Chinese culture for millennia, as is evident from literary and folkloristic sources. The following words of desperate longing, for example, come from *The Book of Songs*, a sixth century BCE collection of Chinese folk poetry:

That the mere glimpse of a plain cap could harry me with such longing,
Cause pain so dire!
That the mere glimpse of a plain coat could stab my heart with grief!
Enough! Take me with you to your home.
That a mere glimpse of plain leggings could tie my heart in tangles!
Enough! Let us two be one.

(Waley 1960:26)

Most modern readers will have little trouble identifying with the yearning that this Chinese maiden expresses, her sentiment being familiar through both contemporary popular culture and scholarship on modern love.

These lines from the same collection add another dimension to pre-Confucian romantic love:

> She threw a quince to me;
> In requital I gave a bright girdle gem.
> No, not just as requital;
> But meaning I would love her forever
> (Waley 1960: 31)

The young man portrayed here speaks of a passion that he expects to last forever, and in doing so alludes to a key feature of romantic love: "the expectation of the lovers that their passion will not die." Romantic love is also prominent in a number of traditional Chinese novellas and in such widely read classic novels as *Story of the Western Chamber* written in the thirteenth century and *The Dream of the Red Mansions* from the eighteenth century (Lee 2010). What was introduced from the West over the last two centuries was not romantic love, but, perhaps, a few of the symbols of romantic love to which Westerners had become accustomed: stylistic representations of the heart, for example, or notions of romantic settings such as tropical beaches, as well as torch songs (Blake 1979a, 1979b).

The idea that marriage should be based on love did not depend on the Chinese learning about love from the West. It was only necessary for the traditional patriarchal structures to decline to a point where young people saw the opportunity to do what they were inclined to do anyway, that is, marry those to whom they were strongly attracted. The propensity to fall in love is, according to ever-accumulating evidence, a genetically based human universal (Jankowiak and Fischer

1992, Fisher 1992). Clearly the emergence of romantic love as a widespread cognitive-behavioral system among young Chinese in the early twentieth century was not a consequence of mere cultural borrowing unrelated to the propensities of the Chinese themselves. We might also note in passing that not everything the West tried to export to China took hold the way love-based marriages did. Christian missionaries, for example, struggled for decades to bring the Celestial Empire into Christendom but they met with very little success.

In the first decade of the twentieth century, a literary form known as Mandarin duck and butterfly fiction gained wide popularity in Shanghai, China's most progressive city. The name comes from the traditional images of mated pairs of Mandarin ducks as symbols of loving couples. The butterfly imagery is related to the fourth-century legend of two tragic lovers who, upon their deaths, are reborn as butterflies. The Mandarin duck and butterfly fiction remained popular for decades despite being disparaged by some of China's most prominent authors (Link 1981). This butterfly literature portrayed love as an essentially spiritual force that drew lovers together despite parental or other social opposition. Though the central figures were invariably represented as extremely attractive physically, their love was never sullied by suggestions of sensuality. Love was seen, in these popular stories of the early twentieth century, as an irresistibly powerful force that would draw two perfect specimens fatefully together, but only on an abstract level. No sex was allowed, not even any kissing.

It was the May Fourth Movement, launched in 1919, which finally put romantic love on the table as a prominent issue of contestation between the young and older generations. This movement, which was initially directed against the Chinese government because of its weakness in foreign policy, was triggered by street demonstrations led by university students in Beijing. The nationwide movement that ensued promoted science and democracy and portrayed Confucianism as an impediment to modernity and a source of China's weakness. A particularly influential novel linked to this movement is Ba Jin's *Family*, which depicts the clash between the Western-educated younger generation of the Gao family and its Confucian elders. The focus of the conflict is the demand of the sons for the right to marry for love, a demand to which the family patriarch won't accede. This novel, which first appeared in 1931, influenced an entire generation of China's youth and helped foster the idea that love was the only proper basis for marriage. Ba Jin's *Family*, given its popularity and prestige, played a significant part in shaping the 1930s as a decade in which freedom of mate choice rose dramatically (Xu and Whyte 1990).

When the Communist Party gained control over Mainland China in 1949, it moved quickly to institute the Marriage Law of 1950, its first major legislative act. This law was designed to give young people the right to choose their own spouses and to equalize the husband-wife relationship so that men could no longer dominate their wives as they had under traditional Confucian principles. In fact, marriages in China's major cities, by the 1940s, had already undergone significant change: arranged marriages were the exception rather than the norm. Couples either found each other absent parental involvement, or the involvement of parents was not so intrusive as to make the marriage a forced or "arranged" one. But in the countryside, the effects of change were slower to arrive. In general, the difference between the way of life in a Chinese city and that found in a typical village is much greater than urban-rural differences typical of Europe or North America. In some cases, this difference was so sharp that even the instituting of the 1950 Marriage Law was not adequate in itself to overthrow the arranged marriage system. The following incident from 1950 will illustrate what was involved in the ending of arranged marriages in China's villages. As ethnographies of other villages by anthropologists Yunxiang Yan and Xin Liu below indicate, some rural areas were still dominated by parentally controlled marriages for decades after the 1950 Marriage Law was passed.

THE END OF ARRANGED MARRIAGE IN A NORTH CHINA VILLAGE

"Heaven is high, the emperor is far away [*Tian gao, huangdi yuan*]." So says a traditional Chinese expression, referencing both the pervasiveness of the central government and its sometimes limited ability to control behavior in the far-flung corners of the realm. In light of this, the Marriage Law of 1950, cooked up in the nation's capital, might not necessarily be expected to quickly sweep away all the patriarchal Confucian traditions that have stood the test of time for hundreds of years. In fact, in a village about thirty-five kilometers north of Beijing, parental intransigence and conservatism succeeded in hindering the implementation of the 1950 Marriage Law until a bold young woman chose to defy tradition, even threatening her relationship with her parents in doing so. This is one of thousands of stories that played out in communities all over China in the 1950s and 1960s as local families struggled to deal with the official challenge to age-old traditions.

The Communist Party, even before its 1949 victory, actually enabled romantic involvement between young men and women by creating new contexts in which they could legitimately interact. During the Anti-Japanese War of 1937–45, the China New Democracy Youth League encouraged participation in party-sponsored mixed-gender activities by adolescents and young adults aged fourteen to twenty-eight. Since the old cultural order had prevented unmarried men and women from interacting, these new contexts amounted to a revolutionary change in social norms. Now men and women could mingle openly, and in doing so, they helped erode the traditional ideal of gender separation.

A young couple whom we will call Zhu Daming and Yang Xiaoying virtually defined the end of arranged marriage for their village in 1951. The girl, Yang Xiaoying, had a well-respected father with a reputation for being intensely reserved and conservative. He rejected the stipulations of the Marriage Law of 1950, believing that the central government should not interfere in a father's right to control his daughter's marriage.

Zhu Daming and Yang Xiaoying came to know each other in the midst of turbulent times. In 1947–48, during China's civil war, control of the village repeatedly shifted back and forth between Communist and Nationalist forces. Most of the villagers supported the Communists, and so, on those occasions when Nationalist troops were present, the bulk of the population fled into the mountains where they had set up a kind of alternate community, complete with schools for the children and other amenities that allowed them to carry on while hiding out from the Nationalists.

The adolescents and young adults of the Youth League focused on supporting the struggle against the Nationalists during the day, but after sunset many of them turned their attentions toward each other, and that's when romantic sparks began to fly. As one elderly villager reported in 2007, the concept of "dating" didn't exist at this time, but young people could, after the meetings, take walks together in the evening. "Walking together," he said, "was the highest form of dating." When asked if on these walks the young couples would hold hands, hug and kiss, he said with a smile, "We did more than that."

It was in this heady and entirely new environment that Zhu Daming and Yang Xiaoying came to regard each other as boyfriend and girlfriend. They spent a good deal of time together while in the mountains, and, by the time the civil war ended and they were able to return permanently to the village, they were in love and had decided to get married.

But Yang Xiaoying's father insisted on the traditional principle of the right of parental control. He had no specific objection to having Zhu Daming as a son-in-law, but he objected strongly to his daughter choosing her own spouse when he, the father, was the one who should have that right. He refused to conform to the new marriage law or to

Xiaoying's wishes. He was adamant that his daughter was not going to do anything so outrageous and unfilial as to choose a husband for herself and that was final. But Xiaoying was equally adamant that she was in love with Zhu Daming and would marry only him.

Xiaoying's household, at this point, turned into a battleground of wills in which neither father nor daughter would yield an inch. Xiaoying's mother supported her husband simply because she didn't want to go against his wishes. She spoke to Xiaoying often, begging her to bring peace to their home by submitting to her father's demands. She even began talking to matchmakers in the hopes of finding another boy whom both father and daughter would find acceptable, but Xiaoying would consider no other prospective husband than Zhu Daming.

Xiaoying's older sister had already gone through an arranged marriage, and this sister also supported the father. She lived in another household, so she wasn't always present, but when she was, she argued vehemently that Xiaoying should do as her father wished. At one point she threatened that if Xiaoying were to go ahead and marry Zhu Daming, she (the older sister) would burn money to the deceased on the wedding day, a gesture that she believed was sure to bring bad luck on the defiant couple.

Xiaoying's father was ordinarily a quiet person who talked little, and in his dispute with his daughter he made his disapproval known with very few words. On those rare occasions when father and daughter mentioned her relationship with Zhu Daming, tempers invariably flared up. So they avoided discussing the issue for the most part. But her father kept her confined to the house, which meant that Xiaoying was frustrated at not being able to take evening walks with her beloved as she had done while living in the mountains.

Xiaoying spent much of her time arguing with her mother, who struggled to convince her daughter to change her mind. But Xiaoying never thought of giving in. At one point she said to her mother, "I am definitely going to marry Zhu Daming. I love him [Wo ai ta]." This was quite a revolutionary thing for a Chinese village girl to say in 1951. Not only was marriage for love a new idea in rural China, but verbalizing love so openly was all but unheard of.

Eventually the story of the young couple and their defiant love reached the ears of some Communist Party members. As a gesture of support for so-called free love (*tan lianai*) marriage, they published details of the Zhu Daming–Yang Xiaoying affair in the county newspaper. The couple was soon famous by virtue of their love for each other. In general, they had the support of not only the editors at the newspaper but their younger generation cohorts as well. The older generation were on Xiaoying's father's side, supporting him and, more generally, the age-old right of parents to choose their children's spouses.

The Yang household conflict came to a boil one September day in 1951 when Mr. Yang was at a village well and overheard some neighbors saying that it looked like Xiaoying was going to marry Zhu Daming against her father's wishes. He had been lifting a bucket of water from the well with a long pole that had a crook on the end. But as he listened to his neighbors talking, he grew furious. Not only was his daughter defying him, but people were now gossiping about it. He put down the water bucket and went back home, carrying the pole with him. Confronting his daughter, he began pounding the heavy pole onto the floor as he shouted, angrily telling her that she could never marry Zhu Daming, he simply would not allow it. Xiaoying's mother was also present, but she just stood quietly next to her husband, saying nothing and staring at the floor.

Xiaoying argued back, insisting that she would marry Daming, until finally, as their words grew more heated and the father more furious, she fled in fear next door to where her aunt lived. The father soon followed his daughter, but he was met at the door by the aunt, who spoke gently to him, trying to calm him down. But he was seething with rage and would not be deterred. While the aunt delayed him, Yang Xiaoying slipped out the back window of the house. Fearful and sobbing, with tears streaming down her face, Xiaoying raced through the village lanes making her way to Zhu Daming's house. The father gave chase, pole in hand, but he didn't catch her before she reached the safety of her boyfriend's home. There, with the support of his parents, Xiaoying found refuge, and the father returned home, defeated. For years after this incident, the story of Yang Xiaoying running through the village crying with her father in hot pursuit lingered in the memories of villagers as a turning point in their marriage system.

And, in fact, one month after this incident, Xiaoying and Daming were married in a simple ceremony, with the couple bowing to Mr. and Mrs. Zhu and then to a portrait of Chairman Mao, which had been set up in the family courtyard for that purpose. Soon after this, a final newspaper story came out, praising the brave young couple for insisting on free choice in their marriage. The feud between father and daughter continued for about a year, but finally he gave in and reconciled with her. From then on, family relations were harmonious. Zhu Daming and Yang Xiaoying enjoyed a happy marriage, eventually, years later, retiring in comfort on Daming's government pension.

COURTSHIP CULTURE IN MAOIST CHINA

Though Yang Xiaoying and Zhu Daming were modern in their defiance of China's patriarchal arranged-marriage tradition, they were traditional in their focus on seeking a stable marriage rather than on the casual pleasures associated with dating. What they and China's youth who followed them embraced was a culture of courtship with marriage as its end goal. In this way, the Chinese approach to marriage was intensely pragmatic. A good marriage for most did not require emotional commitment, sexual interest, or even the development of a sense of friendship between spouses (Schneider 2014). It would not be until the late 1990s, when China's single-child generation came of age, that it became customary for young people to date or to hang out simply for the pleasure they took in each other's company.

The Communist Party's policy throughout the 1950s promoted love-based marriages, but the love in question was supposed to conform to socialist ideals and contribute to the building of the new society. It was not conceived of as a "bourgeois" sentiment that glorified individual pleasures or jealousies. In this setting, familial love and not romantic love was the preferred ideal. Blake's analysis of Communist Party-approved love songs of the Great Leap Forward period (1958–61) illustrates one way in which the authorities attempted to commandeer some of the symbols and themes of popular culture in order to promote collective labor and increase productivity on the new communes. Here, for example, are lyrics from a song about a good socialist bride who, unlike the shy brides of traditional times, does not hesitate to confront the groom's family and friends with a challenge:

> A new bride comes to the village,
> Young men all crowd around her;
> Some hold out hands for cigarettes,
> Some hold out for sweets.
> The new bride just smiles,
> She is neither timid nor hasty;
> She takes from her bosom a production schedule,
> Deliberately speaking to the crowd:
> I have cigarettes, I have candy,
> But we cannot eat them now;
> Whoever beats me in production—
> Ha, come and eat as much as you can.
> The young men just stick out their tongues,
> Yo, this bride sure has pith:
> Okay, you dare to challenge us,
> We dare to take it up.
>
> (Blake 1979:48)

So much for the idealization of the docile, timid bride of Confucian tradition.

The free choice marriage ideal strengthened the position of the younger generation vis-a-vis their parents, and not incidentally helped undermine the authority of the powerful lineages that had long dominated much of China. Just as Confucianism strengthened patriarchal families by subordinating the young, Communist ideology and changes in social organization took away the family's property, a primary source of parental power and authority. In effect, the social reforms seriously weakened Confucian patriarchy.

Though the Communists favored equality between the sexes, it can't be said the gender bias was entirely eliminated through party edicts. Still, the entrenched male bias of traditional China was weakened by the onslaught of egalitarianism called for by the cadres in the years following the Communist victory. One result of the new empowerment of women was an increase in divorce in the early 1950s. The sudden rise in divorces in the first few years following the introduction of the 1950 Marriage Law was unlike anything China had seen before. Women initiated most of the divorces, which resulted in the new marriage law being popularly referred to as "the women's law." Nonetheless, conservative habits prevented the divorce law from being smoothly implemented. In some cases local cadres were unwilling to grant divorces or tried to discourage them by making it difficult for women to take their rightful share of family property when they left their husbands. Most cadres were males and their bias against women reflected both a lingering ideological attachment to patriarchal principles and their material interest in undermining female empowerment. Despite foot dragging by some cadres, however, party leaders at the national level campaigned to spread the word about the right of every individual to choose their own spouse and the right to leave any spouse whom they had been forced to marry. Consequently from 1950 to 1953, the divorce rate soared. After 1953, once many of the women who had felt trapped in unbearable marriages had gained their freedom, the divorce rate dropped back to its traditionally low level.

Since the new marriage law meant that parents no longer had the legal right to choose wives and husbands for their children, the latter were now often on their own in seeking suitable spouses. In urban China, the culture of courtship that increasingly dominated China from the 1930s to the 1980s offered a number of paths through which an individual could find an appropriate mate. During this period, when couples openly spent time together taking walks, having dinner, and otherwise getting to know each other, the focus of their interactions was on the prospect of marriage. But how young men and women came to involve themselves in a courting relationship varied from case to case. Generally the potential spouses would either meet through the introduction of a third party or they would meet on their own, as in the workplace. Rural China in the Maoist era saw the development of formalized boy-girl meetings, usually arranged with the assistance of a go-between. But in both urban and rural communities, when a couple was introduced by their parents or through a go-between they were not obligated to follow through to marriage. Whether their parents encouraged it or not, both male and female youths had the legal right to either continue the relationship or back out of it as they chose. In fact, parents had enough influence that they could, in many cases, squelch a match they considered inappropriate, even in the face of resistance on the part of their son or daughter. In any case, though a parent might convince a child to end a romantic affair, parents could no longer legally force marriage on their children, and for urban Chinese, coerced marriage became a thing of the past.

The Maoist era, the period from the 1950s to the late 1970s, was characterized by a great deal of turbulence triggered mainly by policies handed down from Chairman Mao and his CCP followers. Most adolescents and young adults were not thoroughly caught up in this turbulence until the beginning of the Great Proletarian Cultural Revolution in 1966. Up until the beginning of the Cultural Revolution, students at both the high school and university level were expected to devote their energies to their studies, not to thoughts of love or marriage. And, in fact, high school romances during this period were rare. For university students, romantic activities had to be undertaken either surreptitiously or with careful consideration of whether their behavior would be considered appropriate in the eyes of school authorities and parents. But this restricted atmosphere was disrupted in 1966 with the beginning of the Cultural Revolution.

The Cultural Revolution was carried out in many cases by high school and university students when Chairman Mao Zedong urged them to seize the day and attack senior officials. Mao also instructed the police not to interfere with the revolutionary actions of these young people. Mao and his allies instigated this movement with two main goals in mind: to undermine the more moderate Communist Party leaders such as Liu Shaoqi and Deng Xiaoping; and to promote a transformation in the thinking of the people of China by rooting out feudalistic and bourgeois liberal values. At this time, Maoism reached a fever pitch that obligated everyone to demonstrate his or her commitment to "the Great Helmsman," as he was commonly known. Those who were thought to stray from Maoist thinking or to be less than fully committed in their loyalty to Chairman Mao were subject to criticism, imprisonment, or even death at the hands of the young activists who, calling themselves "Red Guards," set themselves up as the defenders of the revolution.

The years from 1966 to early 1969 were particularly turbulent, as schools were closed and young people formed themselves into Red Guard organizations and, at times, fought against each other in their efforts to demonstrate their superior dedication to revolutionary values. At this time, many students, suddenly granted unprecedented freedom due to the closing of the schools, seized the opportunity to travel throughout China ostensibly to promote revolutionary values but often enough simply to visit far-flung parts of the country.

The empowerment of the Red Guards served to further undermine the traditional ideology of filial obedience, which had already been battered by Communist attacks on arranged marriage and other Confucian institutions. The sweeping away of parents' and teachers' authority during the Cultural Revolution made it possible for young people to engage in dalliances that would not have been possible under more ordered circumstances. Sometimes the anarchic features of this era directly resulted in outrageous acts of sexual violence. In his memoir, co-authored with Judith Shapiro, Liang Heng describes a flagrant, broad-daylight rape by two Red Guards on a railroad coal car (Liang and Shapiro 1983:126).

In another account, a naive young woman, twenty-one at the time, is seduced by her tutor, the first man ever to kiss her. Her ignorance was such that she feared that kissing might result in pregnancy. Her mother, a cold and uncaring woman, beat her daughter brutally when she suspected the affair, but the young woman refused to admit anything. Finally the tutor, fearing that his improper behavior would get him into trouble, took the young woman aside and told her never to come see him again. In the meantime, he wrote a report accusing her of trying to seduce him in order to get a job at the magazine where he worked (Wen 1995:100–104).

Not all Cultural Revolution affairs were brutal or exploitative. A number of young men and women, freed from parental constraints, were able to take advantage of the courtship culture that had risen to prominence in the 1950s in urban China. They actually pursued affairs that resulted in free-choice marriages.

Yue Daiyun in her memoir reveals a poignant story about the possibilities of love-based marriages and the pitfalls of romantic life during the Cultural Revolution. Her story focuses on a female student from

Beijing University nicknamed Laughing Eyes, who, in 1967, had fallen in love with a fellow student whose criticism of a Chinese leader made him subject to arrest. Just as he was about to be seized, the couple fled together to northeastern China where the young man's family lived.

Some two years later in the "Clean the Ranks" movement, the young man was discovered, brought back to the campus, and struggled against as a counter-revolutionary. Laughing Eyes stood by him loyally throughout his difficulties, waiting for him when he was sent to the cadre school in 1969 and placed under the supervision of Daiyun's work team. Finally he was rehabilitated after the fall of the Gang of Four, whereupon the two were married at last, and the husband was given a job teaching Chinese at a university in the Northeast (Yue and Wakeman 1985:216).

THE REFORM ERA AND THE EMERGENCE OF DATING CULTURE

Shortly after the death of Chairman Mao in 1976, China once more began to undergo dramatic change. The Chairman's personality, which for decades had loomed godlike over the nation, finally departed the scene, allowing China's society, including its families, to evolve in new directions. In a period now commonly referred to as the Reform Era, Deng Xiaoping, who took over the reins of power in 1978, pursued policies that downplayed Marxist ideology in favor of more practical initiatives aimed at supporting China's economic development. Deng's reforms allowed families to engage in profit-oriented activities, and eliminated many of the political barriers that had isolated China from the West. The extent of the isolation of the PRC from the West in the 1950s and 1960s had been extreme. In many ways it was not much different from that characterizing the separation of the West from North Korea today.

Deng's economic reforms started out with very limited steps toward a market system, but rather quickly grew to the point where the bulk of China's economy was market-driven. At the same time, China opened its doors to the West. The trickle of foreign travelers who made it to China in the early 1980s, grew to a flood by the 1990s. Companies from Japan, Taiwan, Europe and North America began to invest in joint enterprises in ever-increasing numbers. At this time also, thousands of Chinese students—at first mainly graduate students—began to study in Western universities. Finally, Japanese and Western films and television programs became widely available in the PRC, as did programs and popular songs from Hong Kong and Taiwan. These were soon followed by Asia's Korean wave. This cultural and economic opening positioned China in the mainstream of late twentieth-century globalization trends. It also brought into play four factors that were highly effective in changing the courtship culture: a rise in the availability of wealth, the maturing of the single-child generation, the expansion of urban venues organized around leisure, and a new awareness of courtship and dating patterns in Western societies.

One indication of the new and more tolerant attitude toward romance following Mao's death was the appearance in Chinese fiction of stories centered on themes of love. One of the earliest and most influential of these was Zhang Jie's "Love Must Not Be Forgotten" (Zhang 1986 [orig. 1979]). This short story, as its title implies, is a paean to love and the idea that the only marriage worth having is one based on love. The story, in fact, is tragic, given that the narrator's mother is deeply in love with a man who returns her feelings, but whom she cannot marry. In her diary she writes:

> I am a materialist, yet I wish there were a Heaven. For then, I know, I would find you there waiting for me. I am going there to join you, to be together for eternity. We need never be parted again or keep at a

distance for fear of spoiling someone else's life. Wait for me, dearest, I am coming.

(Zhang 1986:48).

Though her deep and enduring love can't be publicly expressed, her tragedy is ameliorated somewhat by her having loved so deeply and, one might say, purely.

Today urban and, increasingly, rural youth have come to view marriage as primarily a relationship that is expected to provide the couple with a deeply satisfying emotional connection. For example, a blog by a young woman defined love as something of an illusion. The blog states:

> You feel happy when he or she is happy, feel sad when he or she is sad, and you think this is love. You appreciate his writings, like being close to him, even feel ecstasy when he is willing to talk to you. You think this is love. These are illusions. For you, love alone is enough. Yet, love alone is never enough. Love immersed in sweet words cannot stand time and hardship. Something more is needed.

Another young woman tries to integrate her idea of love with pragmatic realities. For her, love needs to be understood as something that coexists outside the family, while only flourishing best when it is developed inside a family. She writes:

> Love comes out of a feeling or emotion. It looks like a mirage: it is beautiful yet too fantastic and unrealistic. However, true love is a long trudge. It consists of responsibility, obligation, and those are far from romantic. This means true love has not begun until you and another form a family. All the love precedes the formation of a family is only the prologue of true love. The rich part of true love resides in and is best created after you form a loving family.

Another woman admits that

> If I am a man's wife I will give my heart completely to him and love him with all my passion. He will be the only man for me and I hope I am the only woman for him. I hate a man who betrays a family [i.e., has an affair]. I want my marriage to be for a lifetime. I want to be a good wife, a good mother, and maintain a harmonious family.

Still another young woman insists that love should flow from an "inner heart and create a loving family or mutual support." It is now understood, particularly in the single-child generation, that a good marriage requires reciprocity, where both partners share and cultivate mutual feelings.

The above quotes highlight the idea that the zone or social space that is best for cultivating the love bond is inside the family. Although love is perceived as an independent force, it is a force that is best nurtured inside of a marriage, rather than, as many Western intellectuals have insisted, outside marriage. For Chinese society, this is a new idea. Previous Chinese generations also assumed that love flourished outside of marriage as reflected in the traditional saying, "Marriage is the tomb of love." But the singleton generation has actually taken to the belief that love flourishes best as a part of marriage. The idea that love is essential to a good marriage and that it is within marriage that love finds its most appropriate home has profound implications for understanding changes in the culture of the Chinese family. Along with this new idea about the importance of private, affective motivations has come a dramatic rise in non-marital and premarital cohabitation (Thornton et al. 2007).

Although everyone assumes that fulfillment of social obligations remains an essential part of marriage, it is no longer singularly central as it had been in the past. China's single-child generation understands the importance of pragmatic interests. But while embracing long-standing obligations it also expects to find, or create, a warm, even intense, love bond. Anything less is considered inadequate for creating a good marriage.

There are two basic coexisting ethical ideal models: the one favored by the generation that came of age before the full effects of the Reform Era took hold and for whom duty and social obligation are still preeminent, and that more typical of the first single-child generation, those Chinese born after 1979 who grew up in the early Reform Era. For these millennial Chinese, trust, shared feelings, and joint activities are the fundamental features of a good marriage.

These millennials, China's first single-child generation, began to reach adolescence in the mid-1990s. As they did so, they brought with them a number of dramatic changes in courtship culture. The lag time between the beginning of China's opening in 1978 and the explosion of change that came in the 1990s, a period of seventeen or so years, represents a repeat of a similar pattern from the beginning of the twentieth century. At that time China opened up to the West following the Boxer Uprising of 1900, and this new openness to the West resulted in extraordinary changes in Chinese society, changes whose full effects were only felt some fifteen to twenty years later, after the May Fourth Movement of 1919. It seems that revolutionary cultural changes initiated by youth are likely to be most dramatic when a young generation grows up in an environment profoundly different from that which its parental generation had experienced.

But the changes in values and behaviors widely perceived in China as part of the rise of the single-child generation are not merely caused by the passage of time. The 1990s were uniquely influential years in China. During this time a number of significant changes reshaped ideas about courtship, dating, and marriage. Two crucial factors behind these changes were the sudden growth of a Chinese middle class due to the rapid rise in economic output, and, as of 1996, the availability of the Internet (Liu 2011). In China there was during the mid-1990s a sense that change, which had already been seen to move with increasing speed, suddenly began to rocket forward in unprecedented ways. What the new attitudes concerning love and marriage on the part of China's single-child generation meant was a fundamental shift in family systems, a shift that had parallels in other countries during the twentieth century.

5 The Preference for the Affection-Based Marriage

We are different from our married classmates, we try to spend every weekend together and do things together. If you value love in a marriage then this is what you must do.

(A twenty-nine-year-old college graduate, from William Jankowiak's unpublished field notes)

Chinese marriages, like marriages around the globe, are trending toward Giddens's "pure relationships," those that are not linked to socially sanctioned obligations but exist only as long as participants want to continue them (Giddens 1992). At the heart of this historic shift is the conviction that a good relationship is identified by the degree of emotional satisfaction present. Given the equality inherent in love bond relationships, there has been an improved status for women.

Giddens used earlier researchers' (Burgess and Locke 1945) conceptual typology that contrasted required role expectations with personal desires. Giddens (1992) and Goode (1963) both thought the familial-duty (or institutional) marriage vs. individual-affect (or conjugal) marriage model was a useful typology to account for the modern family's transformation. The core assumption of the conjugal marriage was the belief that a good marriage was organized around mutual spousal emotional involvement. No longer was the family's primary function organized around raising healthy children or creating an economically sound household. In the new milieu, life satisfaction now includes spousal emotional support.

Lewis, relying primarily on England and Wales data, highlights the new behaviors and social expectations associated with a companionate love marriage. He writes: "By the middle of the [twentieth] century, it was accepted that a more 'companionate' family that stressed the quality of more democratic relationships between adults and between parents and children, over and above the institution of marriage per se, was important to successful socialization" (2001:7). The trend toward egalitarian, emotion-based love marriages is characteristic of changes in Western marriages (Commaille 1983, Brockmann 1987, Hall 1996, Collier 1997). According to Parsons (1964), the fundamental features of the conjugal family are its relative isolation, both emotionally and in terms of economic and other practical concerns, from extended kin: neolocal residence; free choice of mate in marriage; and marriage based on mutual attraction. Finally, because the conjugal family is relatively isolated from extended kin, the emotions within it are intense and the relationship itself is often unstable. Given the new psychological expectations brought to marriage, divorce became more common than it was in the era of the institutional marriage.

The transition from institutional to companionate or conjugal families during the twentieth century did not follow precisely parallel paths in China and the West. The main differences were that at the beginning of the twentieth century, Western families, compared to their Chinese counterparts, were less authoritarian, less patriarchal, and less controlling with regard to the courtship and marriage of their young adults. Given a significantly less conservative starting point for Western families, the shift from institutional to companionate or conjugal forms in the West was less dramatic and less controversial than it was in China. And at the close of the twentieth century, Western and Chinese families were by no means so closely matched in features as to be identical to each other in their most basic or common forms. Some deeply rooted differences continue to distinguish them.

Long-held ideas about appropriate behavior continue to influence behavior, even among the single-child generation. If there is one feature of dating, courtship, and marriage that distinguishes the Chinese pattern, it is the assumption that Chinese parents should be actively involved in their children's love affairs. Arranged marriages lasted in China's countryside well into the late 1980s. In urban China, parental authority was undermined earlier. Although urban marriages are not officially arranged, parents, especially mothers, have exerted emotional authority over their daughters. This can lead to gut-wrenching dialogues between mother and daughter, the latter desperately wanting her mother's approval for her marital choice. This mother-child bond was not as intensely formed in China's former multi-child households. It appears to be an artifact of many mothers deciding to become more intimately involved in raising their only child, which has resulted in the formation of closer mother-daughter bonds. The deep psychological bond only occurred if the mother was actively involved in early childcare. If a grandparent was the primary caretaker the mother-daughter bond was not as intense. Given the strength of this assumption and practice contemporary Chinese marriages fall along a continuum that stretches between a duty-bound, pragmatic, albeit semi-patriarchal structure, and a highly individualistic, egalitarian pure relationship ideal.

The generational transformation away from institutional marriage to a conjugal marriage also contributed to the development of China's new dating culture. A dating culture is distinguished from a courtship culture by virtue of its focus on the simple delight of developing affective feelings with no particular intention to marry. A critical aspect of dating culture is the ability of an individual, male or female, to stop dating one person and start with another with no fear of significant damage to one's reputation. By preferring to "hang out," China's single-child generation not only delayed marriage but also used the time to engage in self-development and to find someone interested in participating in a love marriage. In this way, a dating culture is consistent with the affective values embedded in the conjugal family. It also correlates with the emphasis on consumption and its attendant symbolism with regard to status in reform-era China.

The emergence of a dating culture that focused on fun rather than marriage had emerged in the West in the early twentieth century. By the 1920s, the so-called flaming youth of that era had begun to indulge in casual dating encounters involving light sexual play that were generally focused on fun, not on the prospect of marriage (Bailey 1989).

Willard Waller, in his description of 1930s American university student relationships, distinguished dating from courtship. He argued that dating was different from courtship in that it is focused on "thrill seeking." The men, he surmised, were seeking sexual experiences while the women particularly appreciated having money spent on them (Waller 1937). This wide-open romantic arena, in which dates are many but enduring relationships few, illustrates one way in which a dating culture, with its specific set of norms and implicit values, can be organized. The Chinese dating scene that eventually emerged in the 1990s is different from this in important ways, but similar in that it represented a break from tradition that granted young people a great deal of freedom to explore life's options. Young Chinese, with their continued reference to family interests as well as more restrained sexual ethics, do not value going out with a large number of partners. For most Chinese students this is not an admired pathway to achieve higher social status. Caution, restraint, and propriety are core values that characterized typical dating behavior. This conservatism can be seen as a function of the continuing influence of the family and traditional ideas that make females vulnerable to accusations that they are loose (or qingfu). To a lesser extent, males are also subject to such accusations. When Chinese form a dating relationship, they usually do so with a degree of caution not found in the American system

(Moore 1998, Waller 1937). The pattern of dating for fun may not have led to the free-for-all that emerged in some early twentieth-century Western contexts, but it did have this in common with them: emotions had a prominence in relationships in a way they never had before. Chinese youth are seeking something equivalent to a "pure relationship" (Farrer 2002).

Though the dating culture promotes romantic relationships that are not aimed at marriage, it is within this culture that future spouses often find each other. A dating relationship that emphasizes participants' feelings can lead more or less easily into a marital relationship that is also based as much on affect as on traditional notions of duty. This new emphasis on affect undermined longstanding ideas about the preeminence of males, ideas that were linked to the Confucian tradition and the concept of complementary duties. Both men and women are equally prone to fall in love, and neither is assumed to hold an advantageous position in a relationship based on romantic sentiment. The modern romantic or married couple establishes a world of shared intimacy; it also creates a world in which men and women are emotional equals. Where love rules, neither gender has an inherent advantage. Though there are a number of environments in contemporary China that favor males, the emotional world of the romantic couple is not one of them.

Current patterns of dating and courtship can be viewed through a framework that opposes the traditional (*chuantong*) to the modern (*xiandai*). In fact, young Chinese will sometimes describe a custom or behavior pattern as traditional when the only thing "traditional" about it is that it grants a greater than usual measure of decisionmaking power to parents or reflects some other restrictions on a romantic couple's interactions. A Hangzhou woman, who married her husband in 1979, described her courtship as "traditional" simply because it took place with the participation and approval of her mother and it culminated in marriage. The woman, whom we will call Zhou Qian, was, over the course of a period of years, introduced to a number of young men by her mother, who was an employee at a bank. Her mother's coworkers also stepped in to offer introductions to potential husbands. Most of these introductions went nowhere due to lack of interest, usually on Zhou Qian's part. Eventually, however, a teacher who was a friend of her mother's introduced Zhou Qian to a young man who proved interesting to her. Zhou Qian and her mother met the young man at the teacher's house and, since the two hit it off, they arranged to meet each other again without the presence of any parents or elders. Eventually, after a series of "dates," they agreed to get married. This pattern is typical of what Johnson (1983) labels "semi-arranged" marriages, in which parents initiate introductions but each of the young principals has veto power. That Zhou Qian would call her marriage "traditional" because of her mother's role in it reflects a modern interpretation. Her marriage was not really traditional, since it was not arranged. By the 1970s or even earlier, however, the meaning of "traditional" in Chinese discourse was modified so that marriages involving significant parental input were contrasted with "free love" marriages in which the partners found each other with no parental involvement. This overemphasis on the traditional feature of a courtship and marriage process that is actually quite modern no doubt reflects the Chinese tendency to idealize those customs that can claim to have their roots in antiquity.

As recently as 1990, Xu and Whyte insisted that the city of Chengdu lacked a true dating culture, including contexts within which young people could "link up romantically without adult supervision in a setting that is not defined as leading directly to marriage" (Xu and Whyte 1990:716). However, in the mid-1980s Jankowiak found a kind of underground dating culture in urban Hohhot that existed alongside a more formal, marriage-oriented courtship culture (Jankowiak 1993). The formal approach to relationships of the courtship culture is intimately linked to family interests. This family-centered focus is evident in that those engaging in courtship typically do so with the knowledge of their parents and sometimes by virtue of introductions provided by parents. Furthermore, the goal of a courtship relationship is marriage, and in China may even imply a traditional concern with the continuation of the family line, at least in rural communities. The discrepancy between the underground dating culture of Hohhot and the apparent absence of a dating culture in the somewhat more cosmopolitan city of Chengdu may be a reflection of the difficulty researchers have in identifying secretive behaviors. In any given setting there may be more romantic and sexual behavior occurring than is widely known. Even during the systematically desexualized Maoist era, some couples managed to establish secret romantic liaisons, and underground dating continues even today among high school students who are supposed to be closely supervised. One student from a Sichuan high school explained how her classmates, ca. 2010, were able to meet for late-night hookups on the only floor in the school that had no surveillance cameras.

During the 1990s, the expression *"warwar"* or "playing around" became popular among students as a way to refer to romantic relationships that were not expected to lead to marriage or to last beyond graduation. Naturally there were those who objected to the new pleasure-oriented dating behavior of young Chinese. But these objections carried little weight, at least where university students and other young adults were concerned. At the high school level, most parents and teachers continued to strongly discourage dating or romantic liaisons of any kind. But on university campuses the authorities did little to squelch them. This laxity on the part of university officials was new in the rapidly changing 1990s; before about 1990, students were strongly discouraged from engaging in romantic relationships.

For young Chinese today who are beyond high school age, there is little reason to hide romantic relationships once they are well established. In the Maoist era and to a lesser extent even in the early Reform

Era (ca. 1980–1990), university student couples were likely to conceal their involvement even as their emotional commitment to each other increased. But since the mid-1990s young Chinese have been typically aboveboard about their relationships. Today, even romantic activities that aren't part of an ongoing relationship may be shared via social media or simply in conversation.

When relationships are based on the premise that the emotional needs of each partner should be satisfied above all, the individual is invested with power that is not typical where duty to elders and obligations to the lineage are pre-eminent. In many ways, the single feature that differentiates late Reform Era China from earlier periods is individualism. The individualistic quality that has taken root in modern China isn't extreme in comparison with the individualism of some Western societies, but it is extreme in comparison to the harshly anti-individualistic worlds of traditional China and the Maoist era (Yan 2003, Moore 2005). This is inevitable given that the fun-seeking aspect of dating is fundamentally individualistic. Those who date simply for fun or because the intimacy often associated with dating is in itself rewarding are responding to internal impulses, the very impulses that were powerfully discouraged by both Confucian and Maoist precepts.

Dating does more than merely provide a context within which one can play around or seek fleeting pleasures. As in countries where dating is a longstanding pattern, in China the dating context provides opportunities for men and women to reach understandings both about themselves and about the sort of person with whom they might be willing to spend the rest of their lives. In this way, the dating culture of contemporary China complements or facilitates individualistic expression.

Different individuals will seek different things when they spend time together on a date, but it can be said that a romantic atmosphere in which two lovers feel they are "alone together" even when in a crowd is part of the ideal story for many couples. Images suggesting a romantic atmosphere are largely derived from Western models. When asked to describe romantic settings, young Chinese often conjure up visions of such sites as isolated beaches, tropical islands, and supposedly romantic cities like Paris and Rome.

Romantic relationships thrive on situations in which lovers can focus attention on each other and on the romantic affect that each other's presence brings to life. This focus on romantic sentiment is a striking departure from traditional Chinese ways. As Sulamith Potter and Jack Potter (1990) point out, a longstanding premise of Chinese traditional culture was that individual emotions were not fundamentally important to the social order. Individuals were expected to align their behavior with what their roles required. This meant the obligations of the traditional, duty-based family: the protectiveness and economic provisioning of a good father and husband or the compliance and household maintenance of a proper wife and mother. When the Potters, who lived in a southern village from 1979 to 1980, inquired about individuals' feelings about their parents' choice of marriage partner for them, the common response was: "What I feel doesn't matter." It was understood that the parents had the right to do whatever they thought would be in their or the larger family's interests. In effect, upholding the social order trumped individual considerations. This approach to sentiment, which the Potters referred to as the "Image of Irrelevant Affect" (Potter and Potter 1990:183), may have been to some extent a defensive response to the aggressively anti-individualistic campaigns of the Maoist era, but it also correlates well with many traditional Confucian ideals concerning the primacy of the social order over individual desires.

Of course, the impulses behind dating are not particularly simple or necessarily straightforward. What we talk about when we talk about love is a tangle of features: a longing for acceptance by a specific other, pleasure in the company of that other, and the satisfaction of a sexually fulfilling relationship. Partners may undergo changes in sentiment; what each one seeks from the relationship may not be adequately communicated, with resulting mismatched expectations or otherwise unsatisfying outcomes. The path of true love may reflect individual sentiments, but it does not necessarily run smooth. Dating in China, as elsewhere, consists of certain ritualistic behaviors that couples enact as they get to know each other and seek ways to maximize the enjoyment of their time together.

The interests of parents and other family members do not vanish with the emergence of the dating culture. They continue to be important to young couples, but there is a sex difference: mothers tend to be more effective in influencing their daughters' marital choices. There are, in fact, two sources of motivation that continue to play a part in the way marriages are formed today. Obligations to the family play a part in most young people's lives, as they did in the past. However, the idea that romantic or sexual liaisons should, in and of themselves, be enjoyable, or to use Waller's term, a source of "thrills," now stands alongside the traditional ideas relating to the family.

Singletons in urban China are different in outlook from preceding cohorts, largely because of factors mentioned above: they are the first generation to enjoy unprecedented levels of prosperity, the first to experience extensive contacts with Western culture, and the first to have access to the Internet. Being only children has an effect as well. Though tales of "little emperors" and "little empresses" often exaggerate the spoiled nature of the singleton generation, it is true that having no siblings means that parental attention is not diluted: the singleton child gets it all; he or she also gets all the pressure. A number of young Chinese talk about the weight on their shoulders given that they are, as they are repeatedly reminded, their parents' only hope for a promising future (Fong 2004).

One feature of dating that began in the 1990s that is entirely new to China is the use of online matchmaking sites. As in the West, there are many such sites, most of which charge for their services. Some target specific categories of customers such as white-collar workers or Chinese interested in meeting foreigners. Different sites require different kinds of information from clients, some being more thorough in their quest for data than others. One such service, for example, in addition to basic items such as age, income, and home town also asks for additional items including one's birth order among one's siblings (if any), religion, everyday routines, food preferences, whether or not one likes to have pets, whether or not one is willing to live with parents, and so on.

In addition to online dating, China has also embraced television programs featuring reality dating. The Shanghai-based program *Saturday Night Date* is broadcast nationwide and has proven quite popular. Even more popular is Jiangsa's *If You Are the One (Fei Cheng Wu Rao)*. This date-matching program stirred up a national debate and a bit of soul-searching in 2010 when a twenty-year-old female contestant rejected a suitor who had invited her to join him for a date on the back of his bicycle. Her words, "I would rather cry in a BMW," was transmogrified in the media: to rather cry in a BMW than smile on a bicycle. Although this remark was repeated in various international media outlets as evidence of Chinese women's crude materialistic orientation toward marriage, it is an incorrect interpretation. Less commented upon was the pronounced hostility to the girl's shallow materialism on the part of Chinese "netizens" or online citizens. The unabashedly materialistic proclamation by the *If You Are the One* contestant did bring to light the money factor in China's increasingly wealth-and-status-conscious dating and mating markets. And it also highlighted the new expectation that a good marriage should also include a feeling of love.

The emergence of China's culture of dating has been nothing short of revolutionary. Along with the dating-for-pleasure culture comes a new understanding of marriage itself, an understanding that sees the emotional needs of husband and wife as preeminent. The focal interest of traditional marriage—that an incoming bride supports the household economy and continues the family line by producing an heir—has lost some of its centrality. There are, of course, individual differences in the extent to which any given couple will focus on emotions at the expense of more traditional ideals and there are powerful social factors affecting this variable as well. Urban couples have been quicker to adopt the new marriage ideal than have rural ones, and those born before 1980 are more likely to give traditional values more weight than do those born later.

A recent survey (2010–13) of 110 Shanghai college students revealed that 86 percent viewed love as an essential element for a good marriage. This represents a significant change in attitudes. Compare this data to a 1983 survey: few respondents then named love as an important factor in the choosing of a spouse (Jankowiak 1993).

Certainly many marriages fail to meet the ideal of the mutually respectful, emotionally egalitarian loving relationship that describes conjugal intimacy at its most rewarding. But more so than in the past, young Chinese expect couples to be communicative and to express their feelings within marriage. They believe that these feelings are a crucial aspect of their relationship's foundation. The idea that husband and wife will continue to perform traditional family duties also lives on, but along with these notions about gender obligations are the new expectations about the emotional and communicative aspects of marriage. The current ideal of young Chinese that says husband and wife should seek feelings of mutual affection and respect means that the husband is no longer the dominant figure in modern marriages that he had been in traditional ones. Male-female differences in expectations have not entirely disappeared, even among college-educated urbanites. Men who hope to get married are still expected to have stable jobs (the more prestigious and remunerative, the better) and to provide the newly married couple with a place of residence. On the other hand, women, to some extent, are seen as the emotional managers in the relationship. And wives do want their husbands to be communicative and affectionate. In a survey of 44 females from Hohhot, 84 percent indicated that they thought it "important for a husband to express love (i.e., communicate) to his wife" (Jankowiak 2013). Generally it is wives rather than husbands who take the initiative in encouraging the conjugal intimacy that is at the heart of many modern marriages.

Couples date primarily to enjoy themselves, but also to see if their partner is someone with whom they can form an emotionally satisfying, long-term bond (at least those who are seriously thinking about marriage do so). Where this kind of evaluation is concerned, little distinguishes the interests of men from those of women—except that women are more likely to look for a husband who can facilitate their upward social mobility. Both men and women seek the satisfaction that comes with affectionate conjugal intimacy in marriage. Given their matching interests in this regard, the old male-dominated playing field has been leveled. The demands of an emotion-based relationship weigh more or less equally on males and females in a way that the obligations and duties of the Confucian family did not. The material obligations that sometimes fall on the shoulders of young husbands, given the continuing interest of many urban women in marrying up, is one of the few things distinguishing female from male mate choice criteria.

Obligations to the family are typically played out, or at least they become most visible, when parents see the long-term interests (especially economic) of their son or daughter in jeopardy. There is always a chance that a parent will view their child's object of affection with reservations or even deep suspicion. It is in such cases that parent-child conflicts over marriage are most likely to erupt.

An important factor shaping contemporary marriage in China is the preference for neolocal marriages among urban couples. Traditional weddings, with the movement of the bride via sedan chair to her new husband's home, resulted in the groom's family accepting her as a new household member. This virilocal pattern is still common in rural communities, but for urbanites it is assumed that the bride and groom will establish a household of their own, independent of parents.

This puts pressure on the groom, however, since he is now viewed as the one who must provide the housing for the new couple. One example of parental resistance illustrating this pressure involved a Shanghai woman in her twenties who, in 2007, had fallen for a young man of whom her parents did not approve. The problem was that he was from a poor family and could not even afford an apartment where the couple would be able to set up a new household. The parents were adamant and, though the daughter cried and begged, they refused to relent. Finally she caved in to their pressure and broke up with her boyfriend. Her situation didn't really improve, however, because shortly after this she became engaged to a Shanghai native whose family was rich and whom her parents liked. But eventually they also broke up; she felt he didn't love her and she didn't love him.

Although China's legal system has prohibited parental control over their children's marriage, this case illustrates the fact that the law hasn't eliminated the parents' psychological power over their offspring. Another case offers the same message. A young woman from Zhejiang was strongly discouraged from pursuing her romance with a man she had met via a website and eventually fallen for. Her parents' problem with him was that he was a junior officer in the army and not likely to ever be particularly prosperous. Through cajoling and pleading, they convinced their daughter to leave him, hoping that she would find a more promising husband, say, a young businessman.

In 2008, a wealthy Fujian family took matters into their own hands when they hired a professional matchmaker to find an appropriate match for their daughter who had recently graduated from high school. They owned a lumber business and their matchmaker managed to find a young man whose family also owned a profitable business. Though the woman was only nineteen—one year under the legal age for women to marry—her parents managed to push the wedding through by bribing a key official.

Parents who oppose marriages on the basis of the prospective groom's income are looking after their daughters' long-term well-being. Of course, given the general lack of financial support for the elderly in China, they may also have their own financial security in mind. At any rate, the single most common source of conflict between parents and their children where romantic affairs are concerned is this: the clash between the feelings of the young person and the parents' perception of their child's long-term economic prospects. And, though young people are legally empowered to marry whom they please, the psychological pressure that parents can apply, backed up by enduring cultural ideas about the propriety of yielding to parental desires, puts a great deal of power in the parents' hands. Economic issues aren't the only ones that bring about parental resistance. In one case from Guangzhou in the late 1980s, a female university student was made to feel obligated to give up on the man she loved. It was her father who interfered when he found out that his daughter was hoping to marry one of her classmates, a young man whom the father thought was inappropriate for her. It was neither his personality nor his limited resources that the father objected to, but the fact that the man in question was pursuing a career that would take him out of the country for extended periods of time. This the father would not allow. Though his daughter tearfully pleaded with him to change his mind, he would not. Ultimately she bent to his will and broke up with her boyfriend, though she loved him deeply. The boyfriend was also heartbroken and when shortly thereafter he fell ill, his classmates concluded it was because of the pain the breakup had caused him.

Even today many young Chinese are frank about giving their parents' opinions a good deal of weight concerning potential spouses, some even saying they would not marry someone of whom their parents disapproved. One young man from Xian said he would not marry against his mother's wishes because, were he to do so, he imagined his position would be very stressful. He noted: "I don't want to be like a sausage in a sandwich between two slices of bread" (Moore and Wei 2012:32).

Parents of modest means who worry about a son's or daughter's marital prospects sometimes dedicate themselves to the task of finding an appropriate mate for him or her. Certain public parks have become known as places where middle-aged parents of young singles congregate, sometimes bringing pictures of their offspring with them. Parents may even do this without their children's knowledge, figuring that if they find a good match for, say, their son, he won't object to the method used to do so. Their efforts, however, are not often fruitful, very few of such matchmaking efforts culminating in marriages. The offspring, if they agree to meet a prospective spouse lined up by a parent, often discover very quickly that they have no chemistry and refuse to meet a second time. In the end, these public park gatherings have more to do with placating parents' anxieties than they do with finding their only child a mate.

It isn't only parents who take it upon themselves to try to match up young marriageables. Newly hired unmarried employees are often told on their first day of work about someone in the office workforce who might be a good match. Some middle-aged and older workers seem to cherish the idea that it is an important part of their role to help the courtship process along for any unmarried young adults they may encounter in their workaday world.

There are two social types that have difficulty in marriage: prosperous and well-educated women, and their opposites—men who are not well educated or not financially well off. These types, if they are in their late twenties or their thirties, are regarded as "leftover women" (*shengnu*) and "leftover men" (*shengnan*). Since men are still expected to be at least as economically secure and well educated as their wives, women who have accomplished "too much" in these areas may find it difficult to find a husband. Many men are attracted to professional women who have firm mate selection criteria: he must have a certain income level, must not have relatives in the countryside (which would imply that he has obligations to a large number of poorer kin), and must be able to talk romantically. If a potential spouse does not meet their minimum criteria, many professional women prefer not to marry. Poor and poorly educated men, of course, face the same problem from the opposite perspective. For men, the requirement that most women expect a prospective husband to provide a place of residence is an increasingly pressing problem. As housing prices soar in China, this resource has become more and more difficult to command, and men who have lost out in the quest for an apartment will have a particularly difficult time finding a bride. Adding to this difficulty for men is the fact that many more men than women have been born since China's one-child policy took effect. Though it is illegal to do so, some pregnant women, upon finding out that their fetus is female, will have it aborted. Other parents abandon baby girls by secretly leaving them in public places so that they wind up in orphanages. From here the baby girls are likely to be adopted by Chinese and, less frequently, foreign families (Johnson 2016). As a consequence of these practices, China today is seeing a generation of men growing up who have no prospect of marriage because there are insufficient numbers of women of appropriate age.

Finding a mate whose education, finances, and other qualities are a good match can be difficult. For those with great wealth and extremely demanding tastes, this difficulty may verge on the impossible. The *New York Times* reported on expensive matchmaking services for men who are willing to pay the thousands or even hundreds of thousands of dollars required to locate prospective brides whose beauty, grace, poise, education, and family background meet their requirements. According to the *Times*, there are dozens of firms now providing this service to Chinese millionaires. "One firm transported 200 would-be trophy wives to a resort town in southwestern China for the perusal of one powerful magnate. Another organized a caravan of BMWs for rich businessmen to find young wives in Sichuan Province" (*New York Times* 2013).

MARRIAGE AND GENDER IN RURAL AND URBAN CHINA

Rural China continues to follow different patterns from those typical of the more globally connected and prosperous urban world. For one thing, marriages in which parents take an active part by arranging introductions for their children (that is, semi-arranged marriages) are much more common in the countryside as compared to the city. Also more common are marriages in which economic and other pressures result in women being essentially coerced into marriages that are not to their liking. Pickowicz and Wang cite the case of Li Meidu, a young woman in rural Hebei who had been strongly urged by her impoverished family to marry the son of the prosperous Wei family, a young man who was mentally challenged and otherwise completely lacking in any of the qualities that would make him a good husband in the eyes of his fellow villagers. The pressures from her family were so compelling and the monetary rewards offered by the Weis so appealing that Li Meidu eventually agreed to the marriage, though her demeanor and her behavior in general made it clear to her husband and the entire village that she was only in the relationship for the money—and for her family's sake (Pickowicz and Wang 2002:58). Other women described by these authors agreed to unappealing marriages by being betrothed when they were too young to resist and by beatings or threats of beatings from the woman's father. Patriarchal authority has clearly managed to live on in some parts of rural China.

There is also a trend of women migrating from poor western regions (Sichuan, Yunnan, Guangxi, and Guizhou) to some of the more prosperous provinces of coastal China, such as Guangdong, Jiangsu, and Hebei (Fan and Huang 1998). In some cases Chinese men are also obtaining wives from Southeast Asian countries (Lu and Wang 2010, Zhang 2011). Fan and Huang regard this trend not as a reflection of arranged marriages, but as cases in which, for the most part, women take matters into their own hands and seek to improve their economic status by locating, with the help of professional matchmakers, husbands whose area of residence offers improved opportunities. In general, urban areas are much more prosperous than rural ones in China and rural provinces located close to major coastal cities are more prosperous than those located further inland. The shortage of women, combined with the growing value placed on the monetary economy, has given many young women new resources of power. For example, they have redefined the bride price as something they and not their parents receive. Moreover, they are insisting on a higher bride price. If they divorce, they remain a valuable resource and, unlike their male counterparts, can and do remarry. In the early twenty-first century, rural women in parts of northern China have come to be seen as the more powerful gender (Li 2013, 2014).

More and more rural marriages today are relatively egalitarian. Yan reports from Xiajia village in Heilongjiang province that free-choice marriages gained a foothold in the 1960s and 1970s. This, of course, meant that the marriage law of 1950 didn't come into full effect here until a decade or more after it was officially instituted. Once free-choice marriages were established, however, they became the norm. No marriages resulted in a breakdown in parent-child relationships and young people generally expressed satisfaction with their choice of spouse (Yan 2003). Rural China may lag behind the cities in the speed with which free choice in marriage has become the norm, but there is a good deal of variation in conditions from region to region, with those closer to urban centers showing more of the effects of the modernizing trends than those in remote inland areas of western China.

In Xiajia village, Yan describes a series of changes in the way men and women relate to each other and in parent-child relations as well. Many of these changes accelerated in the 1990s. New houses are constructed so as to allow for more privacy for individuals, which in turn facilitates romantic encounters between young men and women. As in urban China, marriage is seen as a relationship between two individuals who seek a strong emotional bond rather than a basis on which to serve their families' interests or continue the patrilineal line. Even the nature of the dowry and the bride price are transformed in such a way as to reflect the emerging independence of both the younger generation as a whole and females vis-a-vis males in particular.

By contrast, another pattern, widespread in rural China and in Taiwan as well, is characterized by marriages in which the parents play a decisive role. Such a system was described, for example, by Liu in the village of Zhaohiahe in Shaanxi province in the 1990s. Here, according to custom, once two families had agreed that their marriageable children would make a good match, the young man and woman were introduced to each other in a ceremony known as *tanhua* or "having a word." Theoretically, given the tenets of the current law, either the prospective bride or groom could, at any point, have declined to go forward with the marriage, but, according to Liu, this almost never happened. In the words of one young woman, at the *tanhua,* "There was nothing to say. I did not care. It was my parents who asked me to go, so I went. I did not have anything to say. We just sat there, looked at each other, and sometimes giggled" (Liu 2000:63). The giggling of this embarrassed couple is reminiscent of a similar fit of embarrassed giggling by the young bride and groom to be in Hinton and Gordon's 1984 film *Small Happiness.* Again, the rate of change in rural China is slower than it is in urban China, where courtship and marriage are concerned. The exceptions to this can be found in those rural areas where marriage and other social institutions have been drastically transformed due to massive out-migration. Rural migrants in the city face barriers due to their lack of an urban residence card (*hukou*), which is needed to gain access to those institutions that provide affordable services such as health care and education. Furthermore, rural China is characterized by much more significant regional differences in marriage and gender relations than is urban China.

MARITAL DISSATISFACTION AND DIVORCE

Marriages in which emotional fulfillment is attained and in which loving sentiments live on despite family and other workaday pressures are not guaranteed for rural or for urban Chinese. In fact, some marriages in China that do not end in divorce survive on what might be called inertia. The couple may live together, but the sense of deeply shared affection is not a part of their lives. This "going through the motions" type of marriage was more or less the norm in the days of arranged marriages and fairly common in the 1980s and earlier when most marriages came about through family-centered courtship rituals. Today such marriages can still be found, but the emphasis that the new model places on love as the only valid basis for a good marriage means that more marriages are satisfactory. It also means that divorce has become a more viable option than it had ever previously been in China. According to China's Ministry of Civil Affairs, the divorce rate has climbed steeply since the beginning of the Reform Era. In 1980 the rate was about .36 divorces per 1,000 population. By 2012 that rate had increased more than fivefold, to 2.2 per thousand, with about half of the increase occurring since the year 2000. In other words, the divorce rate is not only rising, its rate of increase is accelerating.

China Daily reported in March 2014 that the divorce rate had reached a point where 10,000 marriages were ended every day and the government was beginning to show concern about this trend. The causes underlying the rise of divorce are the increasing prosperity that allows individuals to maintain their own households, high expectations that many couples bring to love-based marriages, and changes in the marriage laws in 1981 and 2003 that made divorce easier. The revised marriage law of 1981 allowed one partner to initiate a divorce if the other were guilty of such things as having an affair, physical abuse, or addiction to drugs or to gambling. And when the 2003 revisions were instated, couples no longer had to get permission from their *danwei* or their neighborhood committee before divorcing. Before then you could only divorce if the local officials approved, something they were all but invariably reluctant to do.

Today, if a marriage is emotionally unsatisfying, that in itself is considered grounds for divorce. This reflects the general trend according to which a marriage is reconceived as fundamentally a source of emotional reward rather than a means of supporting family or lineage. Along with this shift in marital expectations has come a corresponding decrease in the stigma associated with divorce. In effect, the desire to form something equivalent to Giddens's pure relationship is influencing individuals to end their "cold (or dead) marriage." Another factor behind the rising divorce rate is the weakening of the idea that it is acceptable for men to have sexual affairs. Increasingly, professional women view their husband's sexual infidelity as a horrible act, which they will no longer tolerate (Shen Yifei, personal exchange 2014).

Another factor is the presence of domestic violence. In many marriages, when there is a problem, couples tend to first withdraw emotionally and become aloof and indifferent to each other. Quarreling is one way in which couples voice their disagreements. In this setting, women and men can become verbally and physically aggressive. A nationwide survey of adults from 20 to 64 years of age found that the percentage of male-on-female violence was 19 percent (the worldwide rate is 21 percent), while mutual violence was 15 percent, with female-on-male violence being only around 3 percent (Parish et al. 2004). The study also found the risk factors associated with partner violence to be low socioeconomic status, use of alcohol, and sexual jealousy. A separate study found that victims of domestic violence seek help only after suffering abuse (on average) twenty-four times (*People's Daily* 2011:2). Contemporary Chinese marriage, like marriage worldwide, is rich in idealistic sentiments that often contrast with some rather negative realities.

There are other ways in which relationships based on individual gratification have developed in Reform Era China that are not characteristic of "pure relationships" in that they reflect a continuing power differential between urban males and rural females. In such relationships, bodies as sexual objects and romance itself may be commoditized or treated as salable. This is a trend that has arisen since the 1990s with the reemergence of prostitution, which had been suppressed or driven deep underground in the Maoist era. In China's cities, most but not all prostitutes are women from rural backgrounds. In addition, a widespread custom in urban and rural settings is for prosperous businessmen and powerful politicians to take a mistress (*ernai*). Some observers describe the taking of an *ernai* as a near necessity for men who seek to attain a certain level of status in the business or governmental world. A powerful man without an *ernai* invites gossip about his status and his masculinity. This puts pressure on such men to maintain mistresses, the more attractive the better. For example, Sophie Song of *International Business Times* writes of one government official who is gay and in a relationship with a boyfriend, but who has an arrangement with a fake *ernai* who can accompany him on those occasions where businessmen and politicians are expected to bring along their mistresses (Song 2013, Osburg 2013). The majority of men, however, do not have mistresses and those who do are cautious. A thirty-three-year-old man noted: "It is important to hide your affairs from your wife. In the past women may have resigned themselves to their husbands philandering but not anymore—now they do not hide their anger." Some Taiwanese businessmen find it relatively easy to conceal their affairs, as they are able to set up two separate families: one in Taiwan and the other on the mainland. In this type of arrangement wives (as daughters-in-law) are expected to take care of their husbands' parents (2005:425), while their husbands are expected to provide financial support for the family in Taiwan but little else.

In addition to the classic mistress arrangement, there are "temporary marriages" that are the result of migration patterns. Rural married men and women move to the city and only return to their home villages once a year. In these circumstances people form long-term relationships or "marriages" with someone who may or not be married. From a male perspective these arrangements resemble polygynous marriages, while from the female perspective they resemble polyandrous marriages. In fact, they are more equivalent to having a live-in lover who shares financial and emotional support. A rural woman captured the essence of this arrangement when she admitted taking a live-in lover who could help with farm labor. She said, "I'd be crazy if there was no helper, I really have no other way" (Hui 2013:3). In this and in many other ways, Chinese marriage types continue to reveal enormous variations across geographical regions and within social classes.

HOMOSEXUAL RELATIONSHIPS AND FAKE MARRIAGES

The erosion of traditional standards of behavior since the 1990s has also resulted in increasing acceptance of gay relationships. Although gay relationships have been known from traditional literature and lore up until the Qing dynasty (Hinsch 1990), it is unclear how closely real relationships matched those that can be found in fictional sources. A startlingly explicit story by seventeenth-century author Li Yu offers one example of a fictional marriage between a scholar, Jifang, and the object of his affections, a teenager named Ruiji. The scholar Jifang proceeds with his courtship of Ruiji according to the rituals and procedures of heterosexual marriage, including the asking of the father of the young man for his blessing and the paying of a substantial bride price. The couple prove to be compatible and, in fact, quite devoted to each other. Li Yu continues:

> Yet a cloud remains over this otherwise happy marriage, because both men know that the day of separation will some day come when Ruiji inevitably leaves to marry a woman. In gratitude for all of the love and devotion showered on him by his lover, Ruiji castrates himself so that he can avoid heterosexual marriage and remain with Jifang forever. Remarkably, the scar heals into the shape of a vagina. From this time forward Ruiji binds his feet, dresses as a woman, and remains indoors like a virtuous wife.
>
> (Hinsch 1990: 128)

Repression of homosexuality in Qing times and throughout most of the twentieth century forced both gay and lesbian relationships underground. In the Maoist era especially, with its systematically desexualized images of males and females, gay and lesbian relationships could not be made public. With the coming of the Reform Era, this began to change. Today, though gay and lesbian bars and other venues have emerged in China's larger urban centers, same-sex marriage is not accepted either legally or by the majority of the public.

Parents' voices remain as strong as ever in influencing offspring as to whom to marry. The strength of this ideal is so pronounced that homosexuals will enter into fake marriages to please their parents. China's tradition of homosexuality is a history about which most Chinese today are ignorant. Believing homosexuality is a practice that only actors engage in, most Chinese, especially those in the senior generation, remain adamantly opposed to its practice. The homosexual stigma in China, as was the case in nineteenth-century Europe, falls more heavily on males than on females. For example, during the Ming dynasty same-sex lovers were not given the gender identity of "lesbian." Women who were sexually attracted to and liked one another were perceived to be emotionally involved but this involvement was not deemed sexual. For most of Chinese history, female-female friendships were perceived to be a kind of sisterhood devoid of sexual interest. This has not been and is not now the case for male homosexuals. For example, Chinese media constantly assert that male homosexuality is a more dangerous activity, as it poses a greater risk to public health and social stability. No logical explanations need be offered to explain why or in what ways male homosexuality could pose a pressing danger to the social order. It is just assumed that it does. This is not so for female homosexuality, which is seldom discussed at all in the media.

Nevertheless, today there are hundreds of gay and lesbian websites and blogs, and the government for the most part does not try to close them. This is a reversal from an earlier view that lasted at least until 2001, that homosexuality was regarded as a deviant sexual behavior that needed to be suppressed. Today young homosexuals no longer believe or fear they are alone and find it easy to make contacts with potential partners. Although contemporary Chinese have become more tolerant of homosexuality and do not oppose gay and lesbian bars, their tolerance is tested when, as parents, their only child insists he or she is not heterosexual.

Li Yinhe estimates that 80 percent of all gay men will marry, while Liu Dalian thinks it is nearer to 90 percent (Burger 2013:142). It is estimated that there are 16 million "homowives" in China. This term refers to heterosexual women in marriages with gay men. In some cases the woman is unaware of the man's sexual orientation. These marriages have been described as "torture for both the wife and the gay husband" (Burger 2013:143). Burger further notes that many women marry for a couple of years with the intent of divorcing and thereby showing their parents that they respected their wishes.

These contract marriages (*xinghun*) are one way in which homo-sexuals try to satisfy their parents' idea of appropriate marriage while avoiding the awkwardness of marrying a straight man or woman (Zheng 2015). This type of marriage is not without psychological pressure. Since everyone assumes this is a heterosexual marriage the "homowife" is expected to entertain his parents, in-laws, and friends without revealing his true identity. It is a performance that is emotionally demanding, physically trying, and, in the end, deeply unsatisfying.

An alternative to the "homowife" marriage is a *lala* (or lesbian) community family marriage. Lucetta Kam, a Shanghai native who migrated as a child to Hong Kong, entered a Shanghai lesbian family to understand how they formed a viable social identity and enduring friendships, and found life satisfaction and personal contentment. Her sample is small but suggestive. She contacted college-age women who were working in professional white-collar occupations. One of her primary research questions was how lesbians manage to avoid marriage to heterosexual men while not upsetting their parents. She points out that fake marriages continue to be one way to create an acceptable social identity, while privately forging an alternative and more pleasing psychosexual identity. Kam discovered that, among the single-child generation, an accepted new rationale has appeared to justify delaying marriage: They want to grow as individuals and have a higher quality of life. This rationale is similar to one used by heterosexual youth who want to delay marriage in order to purchase an apartment as well as grow as a person.

We found the more interesting part of her study to be her brief discussion on lesbian kinship and household organization. It is typical in Shanghai for lesbians to form households, share rent, food costs, and provide mutual support. Unlike same-sex heterosexuals who share an apartment, the lesbian households also assume fictive kinship identities: One person will become the "father" of the household, while another will be the "mother," with other members becoming daughters to the fictive couple. If there are additional members, they will be referred to as cousins. These roles are initially formed with merriment and affection, but become over time internalized. Household members act out their new fictive kin identity. For example, the mother will listen and give relationship advice to the daughters. Kam notes that these role postures help forge deeper love bonds. Kam does not discuss (perhaps due to the newness of these types of fictive families) what happens when the household breaks up or how long these "families" remain together or whether there is much of a desire, as has been reported among lesbian partnerships in the West, to reproduce and have a child of their own. And Kam provides no discussion of household or "family" conflicts or how these issues are managed.

In sum, Chinese marriage has shifted from an institution organized around a hierarchical, duty-bound relationship into an emotionally based partnership. Women and men expect and desire their marital bond to be anchored in mutual regard and affection. As in European and American cultures, not every marriage achieves this. Still, it remains a positive and intensely desired ideal that shapes spousal expectations and behaviors.

6 Parenting Philosophy and Practice

My mother and I do not get along—she tries to control me and act as
if she has the authority—but she did not raise me. My grandmother
did and that is who I feel closest to.

> (from William Jankowiak's unpublished field notes)

My dad is like my safe haven. No matter what happens I can go to him
to tutor me on schoolwork. He would allow me to sit close to him, let
me sit on his lap...He would often ask for three kisses [laughs].

> (a Nanjing elementary school girl on her relationship with
> her father, from Xuan Li's unpublished field notes)

The Chinese family has long sustained itself on two foundations: the
mutual dependency of its individual members, and as a common prop-
erty-owning unit embedded within a patrilineal descent system. Consequently most Chinese families have exhibited patriarchal and
patrilineal features in the realms of property management and inheritance, as well as in the rituals associated with weddings, funerals, and
the commemoration of ancestors.

The transformation of the family away from its status as a common-
property-holding unit began in the early twentieth century and was
first evident in China's largest cities (Lang 1945; Levy 1950). But then,
particularly under the impetus of 1950s reforms, the family was done
away with as a primary production unit. This resulted in the elimination of inheritable property and with it the leverage that this once gave

to parents. In effect the loss of family property undercut parental power and helped expand the influence of the work unit and other such social institutions...Today, the Chinese family is increasingly an individualistic enterprise whose members are linked together through bonds of sentiment rather than by virtue of their designated duties (Marsh 1996; Yan 2003). The shift in family dynamics away from a duty-based ethos reveals how the corporate and private lives are less analytical models than alternative descriptive frameworks useful in assessing family relationship in different historical eras. In this chapter we will focus less on structural factors and more on how and why affective ties are changing within the domain of parent-child relations. Naturally, parent-child relations are distinct from the relationship between romantically linked individuals. However, there is a similarity in the way positive sentiment has come to be seen as increasingly important in parent-child relations, just as romantic sentiments have come to dominate the way ideal marriages are envisioned. For parents and children, the trend toward an emphasis on affective ties was especially accelerated by the institutionalization in 1979 of the state's single-child policy, which only ended officially in 2015. These changes in urban Chinese families are typical of those evident in a worldwide pattern that has de-emphasized fertility and the power of the elders, and has turned instead to an emphasis on the affective bonds that ideally underlie conjugal intimacy (Goode 1963).

The trends that characterize new parenting styles in China can't be summarized in a single simple sentence. Corresponding with the movement toward more expressive parenting styles is an increase in the ability of women to assert their interests. The enhancement of women's rights, like many cultural changes in China, occurred first in urban families (Jankowiak 1993), and only later in rural areas (Yan 2003; Shi 2009). To date, most social scientists have focused on understanding family dynamics as these pertain to men's and women's social roles, their tacit understandings, and their self-interests. The emergence of affect as a prominent feature of family relationships has been largely overlooked. In fact, there have been virtually no studies of father-child interactions that situate this bond as an emerging affectionate relationship within the changing Chinese family.

In this chapter we will consider the various practices and styles of parenting typical of urban China today. The ways men are re-imagining and redefining the meaning of masculinity stand out as prominent factors in China's current cultural transformation in family relationships. Market-driven reforms that have opened up previously restricted opportunities have helped to validate the changes in these relationships, particularly their affective components (Jankowiak and Li 2016). Here we will compare fathers' and mothers' styles of interaction with what for most parents is their only child. These styles, of course, reflect to varying degrees the organization of the modern Chinese family around feelings of mutual affection.

THE CHINESE FATHER:
A HISTORICAL OVERVIEW

Scholars stress that the Han Chinese father-child relationship was historically based on an ideology of filial piety that required obedience, respect, and loyalty from children (de Groot 1982–1910; Hanan 1988; Freedman 1966). It was also understood that the "father had obligations far beyond that of providing food and clothing and shelter for his [children]." He also had to provide, especially in the case of his sons, sufficient funds to obtain a wife and receive an inheritance (Levy 1968:169). Fathers, for the most part, undertook their duties seriously and strove to economically support and morally instruct their children (Wolf 1972). However, traditional Chinese fathers, unlike mothers, did not generally strive to develop a warm, emotionally charged parent-child relationship. Rather they believed that their role should *not* encourage or tolerate emotional indulgence. They assumed instead the ideal role of a stern disciplinarian (Fei 1947; Fung 1999; Ho 1987; Wilson 1974; Wolf 1972). This stern father posture did not mean that fathers were without compassion or love for their children. In fact, most Chinese fathers felt a deep and affectionate sentiment toward their children (Solomon 1971; Hsiung 2005). But the open expression of that sentiment was constrained by the expectations associated with their traditional role (Levy 1968). Solomon cites a Qing dynasty scholar-official who wrote that a "father loved his child with all his heart, but he would not express it" (Solomon 1971:61). He further adds that this parenting posture sometimes produced resentment and acute anxiety for the child in later life (Solomon 1971:39–61). A Chinese ethos emerged that justified complementary parenting postures: The father facilitated a child's entry into the outside world, whereas the mother provided a secure and loving environment within the home. It was assumed that these roles were inevitable and unchangeable. In addition, it also was assumed this sexual division in parenting roles contributed to producing responsible and ethical individuals (Solomon 1971).

The sex-linked parenting roles depended on men and women occupying different positions within the social structure. By controlling the distribution of the family inheritance, a father could effect a psychological dependency on the part of the child. On the other hand, a mother's parenting style was seen as a result of being considered an "outsider" as well as having a "natural" attachment fostered through childbirth and childcare. Given her lower status in her husband's family, the mother was in a position to welcome a friend and ally. And what better friend and ally could she have than her own child (Wolf 1972; Stafford 2000)? The different access to economic and psychological "resources" contributed to the elaboration of the two complementary parenting styles: the father as a disciplinary provider, the mother as an intimate nurturer.

CHINESE PARENTHOOD: LEVEL OF
PARENTAL INVOLVEMENT

The increased value given to the cultivation of emotional development arose, at least in part, from the emerging belief that it was more adaptive, in the new, rapidly changing society, to raise an emotionally secure and autonomous child rather than an unreflective or suppressed conformist. Parents, through various media outlets, have picked up the idea that a professionally competitive, high-quality (*gao suzhi*) child only blooms when fathers and mothers are skilled in providing parental love and are liberal about granting autonomy.

Lu and Chang's (2013) multisite urban survey found evidence of the transformation in the way Chinese parents approach child rearing. They use a "firm and yet child-centered, egalitarian and warmth-oriented rather than a control [for the sake of control] orientation" (2013:335). Urban parents, and, increasingly rural ones as well, encourage assertiveness and discourage behavioral constraint and modesty (Lu and Chang 2013:335, Shi 2017). Accompanying this shift is the belief that shyness in males is now viewed as a negative male trait, a belief that is quite new in China. In the contemporary social world the extroverted individual is currently deemed the preferred public persona.

An extensive study by Way et al. (2013) on urban child-rearing practices found a fundamental shift toward the importance of raising a morally proper child who also excelled in school. Urban parents understood the "importance of raising a socially and emotionally adjusted child who had the capacity to be self-sufficient and gainfully employed" (Way et al. 2013: 61). This research team also found that low-income mothers thought giving a child more autonomy would allow them more opportunities to thrive (Way et al. 2013). A primary reason for the shift away from a stern, demanding, and uncompromising parenting posture is the reality that raising a single child is easier than raising a household full of children. Parents discovered they could fairly easily influence their child's development without the use of a stern and demanding parenting style (Fong 2007). Their behavioral shift was also supported by the changes in the economy that rewarded the cultivation of nimble social skills as well as individual initiative. Consequently, contemporary Chinese parents have been widely observed to consciously take the opportunity of day-to-day parent-child interactions to promote their children's self-esteem and independence. Urban parents in particular show a commitment to the desire to raise children that are (in addition to being obedient and respectful) happy, healthy, independent, and self-confident. This is the kind of individual they believe will have the greatest potential to become high-achieving (*youxiu*), emotionally well-adjusted, and considerate individuals (Naftali 2009, Way et al. 2013, Xu 2014). Despite the lingering contradictions in parenting values and a lack of a total cultural consensus on child-rearing strategies (Fong 2007, Jankowiak 2011), it is generally agreed that warm, nurturing parents, regardless of their gender, are essential for the development of a psychologically healthy child. In today's China, as in many parts of the developed world where a "psychologized" discourse of child development prevails, it is no longer sufficient for parents to be just financial providers and disciplinarians; fathers and mothers are now required to take on a wide range of other roles, including teacher, playmate, counselor, and friend (Li and Lamb 2013; Naftali 2010; Short et al. 2001).

The shift in parenting practices has ambiguities. For example, Jing Xu's (2014) study of Shanghai middle-class parents of preschoolers found an acute dilemma in their worldview: How to encourage their only child to relate to the outside world? Xu (2014) also points out that parents want to train their child for life's contingencies, while at the same time seeing that he or she becomes a good moral person (Stafford 1995; also see a similar trend in rural Taiwan). Fong (2007) and Jankowiak (2011) in separate studies found that there is an uneasy mix of contradictory values that encourage independence and self-reliance alongside obedience and dependency. So parents find themselves attempting to balance coercion and negotiation in dealing with their only child. For example, a Nanjing mother said,

> Sometimes kids have their own will...you cannot force it....Trying to force him only makes him unhappy and me unhappy as well....My son will ignore you even when you talk to him. When he listens, he still argues with you. He does not follow what you say. It's not like what it was in the past; he listened to everything you told him. Now, he does things according to his own will. Your talking to him is pointless....He has the final say for his stuff.
>
> (cited in Way et al. 2013:66)

Another mother revealed the following insight on her daughter's character:

> You cannot try to control her and tell her what was not allowed to read at all. Of course, even if you do not allow it, she would still do it anyway, but you will have no ways to deal with her. Nowadays kids are just like that.
>
> (cited in Way et al. 2013:67)

This new philosophy toward child-rearing can result in teenagers being less than grateful for their parents' sacrifices. One young woman recalled that as a teenager, "I did not know how to appreciate my mother's love. She was always trying to protect me, but I took everything for granted." She added that once she told her mother she hated her and her mother called her a "devil child." The youth added that as she grew older (at the age of twenty-one) she realized "how deep my mother's love is and how much she has given to me." The new parent-child morality calls for parental responsibility in attending to the child's emotional needs. This can create fragile or asymmetric relationships when an only child feels entitled to accept parental indulgence but is unwilling to reciprocate due to a perception (real or imagined) of parental incompetence or neglect.

The shift in parenting morality is also affecting rural culture and parents in the countryside also find themselves adjusting to the new realities. The availability of service jobs for young females is affecting families' ideas about providing education for their children. Lihong Shi (2016) found that parents often chose to devote their limited resources to their children's education, but in many cases to a daughter rather than a son. The reasoning behind this nontraditional idea is that in the new economy a daughter is in a better position than a son would be to obtain a good job if she has a good education. Thus the family is likely to place its hopes on a capable daughter's future rather than a less capable son's.

The shift in parenting attitudes receives support from popular magazine articles, pop psychology books, TV talk shows, and governmental publications (Kuan 2011). Various media outlets now urge parents to refrain from verbally abusing children or using corporal punishment (Naftali 2009). Some popular publications even urge parents to respect their child's privacy within the home (Naftali 2010). The media outlets argue that a single child should be encouraged to develop as an individual with rights and agency, instead of being viewed as a mere carrier of the family lineage (Naftali 2009). Chinese parents' changing responses to the realities of smaller families is similar to the way Westerners also changed their child-rearing practices. During the twentieth century European and North American societies shifted away from farming to more urbanized industrialized systems. In the process, the size of the family was also reduced. As in the case of China, this provided the essential foundation for a new kind of upbringing (Mintz 2004:77). In China's case, parents broke with the orthodox top-down instructional morality and began to consider a child's emotional well-being as a core element of its individual consciousness. Parents began to accept that a young child has a "right to speak their minds and that the use of violence is an inadmissible educational practice" (Naftali 2009:84).

Between 2008 and 2012, Shanghai newspapers were full of stories about how rural teachers or parents had physically injured a child trying to get him or her to study better. The message behind these morality vignettes was clear: the good parent uses restraint, kindness and guidance to get the best from a child. Taken together these publications and the accompanying public discourse are indicative of the government's effort to change the demeanor and thus the quality of the parent-child relationship. There is evidence that media encouragement did not cause the changes in ideas about how best to raise a child but followed them. Jankowiak's (1993) 1980s research reveals that many of the media assertions prominent in the 2000s about the "new changes" had already taken place in a number of northern Chinese urban families. For example, throughout the 1980s, many unmarried men admitted "loving their father, but not liking him." And they would often add that they would be a different kind of parent to their child. The media's onslaught has given voice to what had been a gradual shift in parents' understanding of what a good parent is. Because Chinese parents, much like Western parents, want to produce children who are self-controlled, empathic, caring, capable of self-expression, and authentic (Lindholm 2001), parents are more than ready to adjust their parenting behavior when they see the benefits of the new ideals.

Differentiated interaction styles of fathers toward sons as opposed to daughters in Chinese families have been well-documented, and have often been ascribed to the agrarian origin of Chinese civilization. In China, as in other traditional agrarian societies, male heirs have long been favored because of their greater potential to provide labor to the family, a vital economic asset in a farming society (Li and Lamb 2013; Lu and Chang 2013; Strom, Strom, and Xie 1995). While enjoying privileges, however, sons in Chinese families—where paternal concern and strictness are often synonymous—receive more control, more harshness, and less demonstrated affection than do daughters. This difference is a reflection of the higher standards that fathers aspire for their sons to reach, and the key gender role they are expected to follow. In contrast to the aloof posture directed at sons, fathers, especially those in prosperous or well-educated social classes, preferred their daughters to develop more emotionally involved relationships. They were therefore likely to treat their daughters with leniency, indulgence, and tenderness (Lu and Chang 2013).

In addition to being gender-sensitive, Chinese fathers typically adjusted their parenting style as a son grew up. Many scholars have noticed the stark contrast in the affective climate of parent-child interactions in Chinese families before and after the child reaches "the age of reason" (*dongshi*) (Chuang and Su 2009; Jankowiak 1992; Putnick et al. 2012; Wolf 1972). Despite the absence of an exact cut-off point, it is generally believed that this transition takes place around the time that the child starts school, that is, at approximately six years of age (Fung 1999; Ho 1988). However, Fung's research (1999) also found many Taiwanese professionals who were actively involved in shaping their toddler's behavior in order to prepare them for preschool.

The national media and governmental directives did not really launch or lead the shift toward a more emotionally supportive parenting style. The Chinese media and government institutions actually followed an already developing cultural trend, rather than leading it. The current public media stress on parenting represents the formalizing of a well-established grassroots change in parenting attitudes and behavior.

Wives also have strong influence over their husbands' behavior. It has been extensively documented in the fatherhood research that men's involvement in childcare is sensitive to their female partners' gender ideologies (Cowan and Cowan 1992). The vast majority of the new generation of Chinese women, often raised as singletons themselves, expect their husbands to assist them in childcare. Furthermore, they are not generally reluctant to voice their wishes during the dating and courtship period, and to continue their advocacy once they are married parents. In interviews, urban Chinese women, whether dating or recently married, overwhelmingly assert that they expect their mates to help with early childrearing. And in contemporary urban China, the men themselves expect to become involved, too. The men's accommodating position on childcare may be an indication of their respect for their wives' expectations and their readiness to please them in order to maintain an emotionally intimate marital relationship. We suspect that Chinese men's eagerness to be involved in childcare tasks, especially when their children are in the early infancy and toddler stage (when childcare for some may seem most tedious and unrewarding) is driven at least in part by the motive to support and please their wives. The wives, in turn, can be expected to reward their husbands with verbal approval or physical affection as recognition and acknowledgement of their efforts in marital courtship (Jankowiak and Li 2016). In time, however, men with a single child may well develop deep attachments to him or her and become involved for no other reason than the fact that they find doing so fulfilling.

Kwok et al. (2013) found that in Hong Kong a father's behavior could result in positive outcomes for a child's development and that poor parent-child relationships can be quite detrimental. Xu and Zhang (2008) quoted a respondent who recalled his father as "competent, reliable, frank, tolerant, and brave, but also as stubborn, inflexible, non-creative, proud, and distant" (Li and Lamb 2013:32). Research found a relationship between a father's involvement and his child's enhanced cognitive development and noted that involved fathers often stimulated their child to outperform peers. "Likewise an observational study of seven-year-olds in Shanghai showed paternal nurturance was related to cooperative peer play" (cited in Li and Lamb 2013:30).

Elsewhere, Hu et al. (2009) report that: "warm, understanding parents tended to have children who were more empathic in early childhood" (cited in Li and Lamb 2013:30). The emotional shift in parenting posture also influences the way a child manipulates his or her parents. For example, Kuan reports that if a child wanted to get out of going to a specialty class, he or she would have a better chance asking their father (2011:85). Mothers believe their husbands are "too casual" and too inclined to go "with the flow" and don't do enough to effectively guide their only child (Kuan 2011:85). A male child aptly summarized this difference in parenting when he blurted out: "My father is the best. Mom is a meanie, doesn't let me do this and doesn't let me do that" (Kuan 2011:85).

Special problems arise for those families in which the parents have migrated to the city—as tens of millions of rural Chinese have since the Reform Era began. The increasing inability of Chinese migrant fathers to regularly interact with their children is having profound negative consequences. When a rural migrant moves to the city, he or she can improve income and livelihood in general. But it is increasingly clear that the disruption of parent-child ties that this entails will often result in real psychological costs for the children who are left behind. Although migrants can bring their children to work with them, they must pay additional educational costs to send them to school in the city. Lacking sufficient funds, the migrant families often send their children back to their home village to be educated. This strategy is likely to have psychological consequences. Father-absent families, compared to father-present families, have more problems with children who lack self-control and who are considered by their teachers to be "troublemakers" (Mischel 1958, Choi and Peng 2016). Other research has found that Chinese fathers who migrated had "left behind" children who are "more inhibited, anxious, and depressed than those who lived with their fathers" (Chen et al. 2009). Chen et al. (2005) also found that a father's absence has more of a negative impact on sons than on daughters. For example, parental indulgence, overprotection, and rejection were more strongly associated with boys than with girls (cited in Li and Lamb 2013:31). Xue Zhao et al. (2014) also discovered that male, but not female, migrant students were more rebellious and performed worse on school exams. Finally, Zhang's (2009) survey on Mainland Chinese youth found them more blunt and forthright in voicing critiques of their parents' behavior, something a previous era's youth would have been uncomfortable expressing.

STYLES OF PARENTAL CAREGIVING

Over the last twenty years or so there has been a strong inconsistency in men's and women's parenting styles. This gender difference includes the following: when women hold a child, they typically hold it close to their body, while men usually hold a baby with arms extended either upward or outward away from their body. Mothers and fathers also differed in the patience shown toward a stubborn child who refused to move. The common response of the Chinese parent is to call out the equivalent of "goodbye" (*zou*) and walk off. Usually the child panics over this threat of abandonment and quickly follows. Although both men and women strive not to use force in motivating their child to move, they are also not above abruptly picking up the child. Significantly, men and women differed in their ability or willingness to wait out a stubborn child's refusal to move. In the twenty-seven incidents of child stubbornness Jankowiak observed (among eighteen mothers and nine fathers), the women were willing to wait longer than the fathers in this bluffing game. Fathers never waited more than five minutes and usually three or fewer minutes before they would return and pick up the child. Mothers would typically be willing to wait more than five minutes.

Men and women also differ in the style used to walk with their child. Women, for example, rarely walk ahead of their child. Rather, they prefer to coach by standing three to four feet behind. The few instances where a mother walked ahead were when the child refused to move forward and the mother wanted to move it along by threats of abandonment. Men, on the other hand, use a different walking style. They usually walk ahead, and not behind, the child, thereby allowing for greater physical distance to grow between parent and child. There appears to be a degree of emphasis on the independence of the child on the part of the fathers. One father allowed a three-year-old child to wander more than thirty yards behind him, something most Chinese mothers would not do. The age and sex of the child did not affect the parents' walking style. Urban fathers allowed young girls to wander just as much as boys, whereas mothers stood just as close to a boy as they did to a girl. Men's concern with teaching independence is also evident in how they interact with their child at a play court establishment. Jankowiak observed that mothers (116 out of 147, or 79 percent) overwhelmingly paid extra to go inside and be closer to their child; whereas fathers (89 out of 113, or 79 percent) preferred to watch intently, from outside the play area. Significantly, in 2007, Jankowiak witnessed on four separate occasions a mother of around thirty years of age walking quickly ahead of her child with the child trying to catch up! Although not representative or typical of the majority of urban Chinese mothers' parenting styles, it is suggestive that some women are changing their parenting practices, perhaps in response to China's renewed emphasis on personal achievement.

Another cultural continuity is in the style of conversation. In the 1980s a pronounced difference existed between mothers and fathers in verbal interactions with their children. If an urban mother is holding a young child, for example, she rarely talks to it. However, as soon as the mother starts walking with the child, she breaks into a mode of continuous verbal coaching toward the child. The verbal stream acts to "hold" her child in check. Unlike urban mothers, Chinese fathers will talk to their child. Many fathers continue to converse as they walk with their child. The conversation revolves around teaching the child something, however, or commanding it to hurry up. The style in which a father commands differs from that of mothers, who typically never stop talking. The father issues commands in rapid bursts, two or three times, to signal the child to move faster. Fathers, in short, do not attempt to use a cradle of sound to communicate closeness or authority. Instead they point out and comment on specific features around them. Regardless of social class, mothers use a harsh and abrasive tone when they address a child of one to six years old. Fathers tend to use a softer tone. Fathers are especially affectionate and openly express this affection to older infants. For instance, Chinese fathers, throughout the 1980s, frequently kissed infants on their exposed buttocks. (In the 1980s urban Chinese did not use diapers but preferred to dress their children in special pants that have an opening in the crotch.) After 2000 this behavior seemed to diminish or disappear, perhaps due to the preference for the use of diapers when taking the infant out in public. As a child enters late childhood (three to six years of age), parents become sensitive to possible gossip over expressing physical affection toward their children. Thus fathers in public, but not necessarily within the home, are reluctant to actually hug a child who is over six years of age. This is especially true in father-daughter interactions. A father told Jankowiak that "sometimes I might want to but I am afraid that people might think I like [xihuan, i.e., sexually] my daughter too much." Another father admitted that he sometimes hugs his ten-year-old daughter but only in the privacy of his home. On the other hand, we observed mothers repeatedly hugging sons or daughters within the home. In contrast, once the child enters the first grade fathers follow the prevalent social conventions, and begin gradually to restrict the frequency of physical affection shown toward their child in the home. In public, however, fathers, as they walk down the street, will typically hold a child's hand. Mothers, once a boy or girl passes puberty, also become more restrained, albeit less so, in their expression of physical affection (Jankowiak 2011).

Although men and women differ in the frequency in which they perform caretaking duties, there is no noticeable difference in the way they perform routine maintenance functions. We observed countless instances in the public park when a father, alone with his child, aptly performed basic childcare duties: wiping a dirty face, slicing food and feeding the child, unwrapping a popsicle or buttoning and unbuttoning a child's clothes. Whenever a child was with both parents, it was assumed that the mother would perform all the necessary caretaking acts, the same acts she performed within the home. This is especially so if the child becomes cranky and starts to cry, a behavior that immediately activates the mother's involvement as it quickly disengages the father's interest. Moreover, in spot observations, Jankowiak noticed that the child looks at the mother more regularly than he or she does at the father. For example, 3.6 glances per 60 seconds were counted for the mother; whereas on average the child looked at the father 1.6 times per 60 seconds. This suggests a continuation in the sexual division of labor as it pertains to parenting behavior. These sex differences in parenting behavior appear to be widespread in China. In a separate study, Susan Short (et al. 2001) found a similar pattern in a four-province study. Short notes that "mothers emphasized the day to day component of caring for children—giving them food and drink, dressing them, teaching them to be good, starting their education and arranging their daily lives" (Short et al. 2001:922). In contrast, the "fathers were responsible for the family's financial security and for mediating relationships within the household" (Short et al. 2001:922).

Men's and women's caretaking behavior does not change noticeably within a more private domestic setting. Whenever a child is sick, for example, it is the mother who cares for it. It is the mother who dresses the child for school and it is the mother who scolds the child when it is bad. The father remains aloof and only enters into the disciplinary role when something serious occurs. A 2008 survey found that the mother continues to be the primary disciplinarian within the family. Every singleton interviewed (forty-six in all) readily recalled being hit by their mother and seldom by their father. This is consistent with the work of Shwalb et al. (2013) concerning East Asian family dynamics. They also found a region-wide shift whereby fathers are more nurturing, whereas mothers are both nurturing and the family's primary disciplinarian. Chu and Yu's (2010) survey of parenting behavior in Taiwan also found a similar shift: mothers were more likely to be disciplinarians than were fathers.

Another behavioral continuity across generations is the way Chinese fathers in public prefer to engage their children in activities—such as playing pool, rowing a boat, rollerblading, and going to the zoo—which encourage creativity and independence. In the domestic sphere, they adopt a more reserved yet still involved stance. For example, they often discuss with, tease, and occasionally wrestle with their child inside the house. Also, a husband is typically ready to help his wife, if she is momentarily overburdened by work or beside herself in anger with the child. This pattern is not unique to northern China (Jankowiak 2011). Short and colleagues found a similar pattern in central China (Short et al. 2001:922). On the other hand, the mother's parenting style in both public and domestic spheres does not change. She remains the primary caretaker who is, though this may seem contradictory, always the nurturer (Lamb 1987). Furthermore, mothers organize activities designed to protect and nurture the child against unseen yet potentially harmful forces, thereby promoting and securing an intensely close emotional bond that normally continues well into adulthood. Significantly, although women often vociferously complained about their husband's lack of support and assistance in performing household chores, most women are willing to overlook this, provided the husband remains steadfast and loyal to her and the family. This sentiment was aptly acknowledged by a thirty-nine-year-old Nanjing woman who, with disgust, noted that her husband "does nothing around the house. He does not help with the chores or ordinary child care" (Li and Lamb 2013). For urban Chinese mothers of every generation, childcare duties are presumed to be sex-linked duties, a linkage considered to be natural, normal, and beyond critical discussion or evaluation.

MOTHER-CHILD AND FATHER-CHILD BOND

A primary means by which Han Chinese women in Imperial and Republican China attempted to protect themselves from a hostile mother-in-law and often an unsympathetic husband, was to foster an intense emotional dependency with her children so that, once grown, they would take care of her (Wolf 1972). It was the mother who was the primary educator of very young children. She set the goals, molded behavior, and forged the intellectual and ethical identity of the culture's next generation. Margery Wolf, in her study of contemporary urban life in the PRC, observed that the recent socialist changes no longer make it necessary for women to foster this type of parent-child dependency. Furthermore:

> The uterine family has disappeared because the need for it has disappeared. Urban women do not express the same degree of anxiety about their old age that they used to. Young women work and expect to receive a pension, older women who do not have pensions are assured by the government that they are cared for.
>
> (1985:207)

Contemporary research, however, continues to find the presence of a close mother-daughter bond. It persists, however, for a different reason: the continuing preference for intense emotional intimacy exists for its own sake, rather as compensation for the absence of a female-centered kin support system. Thus, mothers continue to exercise tremendous psychological control over their offspring. For example, in an offspring's mate selection, it was inevitably the mother, and not the father, who was the deciding force. Middle-aged men and women frequently confided to us that their emotional involvement with their mothers remained remarkably strong after their marriage and throughout their adult lives. In the 1980s the intensity of the emotional adoration was expressed to Jankowiak by several college students in their twenties, who permitted him to read sections of their diaries. One twenty-six-year-old female student wrote: "I love my mother very much, from my heart. She has given me too much, both knowledge of society and science, and knowledge of life. She has taught me how to encounter difficulties. Now she is ill, I wish it was me instead." A twenty-year-old young man wrote, "In the evening I write to my mother. I miss her very much, and I can imagine how much she misses me. I've just received a letter from my mother. She told me she is very healthy and pleased. She said she misses me and hopes I can go back home on the holidays."

A nineteen-year-old student, who was suffering from a cold, acknowledged that "I think of my dear mother. If she was here, she could cook delicious food for me and comfort me. But here 5,000 miles away from home, who could be as dear as my mother?" Finally, a twenty-one-year-old male student recorded rather bleakly in his diary "another Sunday of loneliness and restlessness. I'd rather be a bird, then I could fly back home and see my mother."

Jankowiak's later research found little had changed: Students continued to share each other's letters from home. Fathers continued to stress the importance of study, hard work and accomplishment, while mothers stressed the importance of eating well. (Food, besides being literally nourishing, also provides a symbolic statement of concern for an individual's well-being.) This is consistent with psychological research reports on European and US parenting practices that found fathers compared to mothers tend to provide better identity models (Shulman and Klein 1993) as well as differentiating more between sons and daughters (Lytton and Romney 1991).

A nineteen-year-old student admitted that her mother had listed all the foods she should and should not eat depending upon the time of year. When her roommates read her letter, they all agreed that she had "a mother who truly loves you." A twenty-year-old student revealed the following letter from her father, who did not mention food but rather how she should organize her day. He wrote that it should "begin with physical exercise, study of literature, then vocabulary words to be followed with a ten-minute rest and then read some more." She noted that her father thought it critical to master the subject so she would be a success in life. The different parenting styles seem to have affected how an offspring thought about each parent. Another example of parent-youth interaction can be found in the story of a female college student who wanted to attend a graduate program in Shanghai while her mother preferred that she go to a university in Xian. After much discussion that included an email from a professor working in Shanghai who did not think the Xian university was that good, the mother agreed to let the student go to the university in Shanghai. In this young woman's case, it was the mother and not the father who held the greater authority. Throughout the 2000s, as in the 1980s, the father continued to be regarded as loving and concerned, albeit at times he seemed the more aloof parent, while the mother was perceived to be more nurturing and thus for the singleton generation the more loving parent.

The research is mixed concerning the degree to which fathers have actually changed their behaviors. Li and Lamb (2013) and Jankowiak (2011) find there has been, especially among the college-educated, a fundamental shift in the way fathers interact with daughters. In contrast, Tam and Chan (2009) report that Hong Kong fathers were seen as less warm than mothers, and Skek (2000) argued that youth found it easier to talk to their mother rather than their father. Fong and Kim's research (2016) in northern China also found that fathers were perceived to be the more stern disciplinarians who only got involved in serious offenses. Further, fathers cared mostly about education and were harsher in correcting what they thought was a child's poor study habits.

In contrast, Li's (2013) Nanjing research found that the father in many families had a good relationship with the daughter. A teenager told Li: "My father is like a safe haven. No matter what happens I can go to him and he can tutor me on schoolwork. He would allow me to sit close to him, let me sit on his lap, make something up. He is not happy with one kiss. He wants three [laughs]." Another father never criticized his daughter when she made a mistake on an exam but would calmly explain how to do it better. Still, Li's research also found a number of fathers who were aloof and indifferent to their child's educational development. A mother noted: "It seems to me he seldom cares about the child…he never asks about her." Li's Nanjing findings are consistent with Jankowiak's (1993, 2011) Hohhot findings. And yet the discrepancy depends upon the type of question or behavior under consideration. Kim and Fong probed how fathers responded when there was a serious problem with household behavior or school performance. Jankowiak and Li focused on less stressful daily interactions. The different data sets are reporting different memories about actions in different domains.

In most Chinese families, the mother continues to be the glue that binds the family together. She is the center of the communication network. Through visits she becomes the focal point for news and a pivot for influencing various kin opinions and actions. For reasons other than simple fear of a vengeful mother-in-law or hostile spouse, the emotional bonds between mother and child formed during infancy and the early childhood years are maintained. These bonds are sustained, in large part, through a Chinese tradition that legitimizes and promotes in practice an intense lifelong emotional bond between mother and child (Solomon 1971, Pye 1985, Hsiung 2005). It is a bond that is idealized in literature and in conversation as a celebration of harmony, remembrance, and enduring love (Link 1981). Moreover, the intensity of its expression signifies to every Hohhotian the continued importance, influence, and power of the Chinese woman.

THE NURTURING FATHER

The shift in ideal images of the father can be symbolized by the difference in tone between the formal Mandarin word for father (*fuqin*) and that for the term that might best be translated as "daddy" (*baba*). The former kin term implies the sort of responsible yet aloof figure of the past (as represented, for example, by the patriarch of the Gao family in the Ba Jin novel *Family*), while the latter suggests a more affectionate and emotionally involved paternal figure. This shift in ideals has been noted by a number of researchers (Jankowiak and Li 2016). Comments from fathers, mothers, and children indicate that Chinese fathers are departing from the traditional posture of someone who fulfills paternal responsibilities backstage to parental figures who are now becoming more present in the foreground of daily childcare. They are often particularly assertive in contributing to the child's educational development (Jankowiak and Li 2016).

In addition to providing increased assistance in childcare and companionship, Chinese fathers are transforming their parenting persona away from the stern authority figure of the past toward a figure of warmth and expressiveness. This change has been elaborated in Qiong Xu and Margaret O'Brien's study (2014) on Shanghai father-daughter dyads, and is also visible in Li's, Jankowiak's, and Moore's samples. A mother from Nanjing, recalling her instructions to her offspring, said that whenever her daughter "makes a mistake on the exam because of sloppiness her father would not become emotional but calmly instruct her"; and, according to another woman from the same city, "when it comes to learning time he would help her [the daughter]. He would never shout at her" (Jankowiak and Li 2016).

The preference for closer, more emotionally intimate father-child relationships as the new parenting ideal is yet to be fully embraced by all Chinese men. Interviews and observations with numerous Chinese parents suggested that the fundamental aspects of being a mature Chinese male—displaying competence and control of self, being an effective family provider, and a source of the family's moral authority—have never disappeared entirely from the fatherhood ideal (Jankowiak and Li 2016). While Chinese fathers are highly devoted to the development of their children, the acceptance of the new "warm father" model varies greatly from family to family, resulting in differences in ideas about appropriate proportions of financial investment and emotional involvement in the household. Rural patterns differ from urban ones where ideas of the father's role are concerned. Among rural migrants to the city, fatherhood is seen as largely based in providing for the family financially. Seeking success in business is one way in which such migrants seek to be good fathers (Osburg 2013). There are those among the working class who, in light of their limited incomes, attempt to compensate for this weakness by expressing paternal affection toward offspring and in general being emotionally involved in their families. Those who have secure middle-class incomes, particularly men in the professions, often strive to be all things to their children, combining financial security on the one hand with strong affective ties to their children on the other.

CONCLUSION

The reevaluation of customary kinship obligations, conjugal expectations and duties, and parent-child interaction are closely intertwined with China's large-scale political and socioeconomic changes. However, these cultural shifts cannot be attributed solely to the socialist transformation of China's urban infrastructure nor to the subsequent Reform Era changes. Lang's (1945) Shanghai study and Whyte and Parish's (1984) urban survey found that many of the domestic changes were already underway prior to the 1949 Communist Revolution. At the same time, the changes in the contemporary urban Chinese family's organization, instead of bearing signatures from traditional Chinese culture or socialist society, seems to have occurred in conjunction with a worldwide pattern that is inclined toward the formation of a nuclear or conjugal family in which interpersonal interactions (especially spousal interactions) are characterized not by detachment but by emotional expressiveness.

This trend toward emotional expressiveness within the family is consistent with Goode's thesis concerning family transformations. According to him (1963), urbanization and industrialization brought about basic changes in the role of emotion within the family. These forces had an impact in twentieth-century China, as did the egalitarianism promoted by the Communist Party. Then, the emergence of the competitive market economy in the Reform Era promoted a spirit of individualism that itself helped change the way masculinity is conceptualized and performed (Jankowiak and Li 2016).

7 | Parents, Adolescents, and Emerging Adults

I have a very strong desire to express myself. So I feel bitter inside. I think parents should be the first people I go to talk to. I want to tell them things that happened to me. But…they never talk to me. They only talk to each other. I feel I'm isolated. My parents made me feel lonely. They discuss everything together and they leave me aside. That's how I feel. I envy children who have parents willing to communicate with them.

(A twenty-year-old Beijing male commenting on his relationship with his parents, from Yuzhu Sun, unpublished paper)

Those nights on the mountain alone I thought I would die. I started to reflect on my life and I realized there was more to life than money and fame. I resolved to become a better person.

(An eighteen-year-old youth reflecting on his experience trapped in a mountain landslide, in Jankowiak 2004)

The dramatic changes that Chinese families have undergone over the past century have weakened a number of traditional family ideals and practices. May Fourth-inspired reactions against Confucianism and, later, the Maoist emphasis on gender equality went a long way toward undermining entrenched ways of thinking about parent-child and male-female relationships. Here we will consider the way in which these changes have had an effect on the adolescents and young adults of modern China. Adulthood, as a life stage, can be marked in terms of three attributes: being responsible for one's actions, being capable of independent decision-making, and being financially independent (Schlegel and Barry 1983). For centuries Chinese society was organized around thick, interdependent personal ties or social bonds, sometimes referred to as collective ties. But a number of factors in twentieth-century China changed this. The tumultuous days of the May Fourth Movement and the Chinese civil war, followed by a series of mass movements in the 1950s and 1960s, reordered Chinese lives in unprecedented ways. Finally, the one-child policy and the single-child generation that resulted from it have encouraged a degree of individualism that makes Chinese adolescence and young adulthood startlingly different from what these statuses were in the past. In effect, adulthood today is not established by such recognized and predictable social accomplishments as marriage and parenthood, but rather by criteria that are less easily identified and more subjective. The culture's shift away from fulfilling specific sanctioned role performances toward an acceptance of a more personalized or idiosyncratic view of adulthood has had profound consequences for the Chinese family. This does not mean that parents no longer have significant influence over their offsprings' lives. Most parents still do. But it does mean that Chinese youth now inhabit two often competing social and ethical universes: one oriented toward self-development and the other toward upholding parental aspirations. In this chapter we will probe some of the dilemmas and responses that arise from embracing these two universes with their sometimes contradictory ethical principles.

COMING OF AGE OF THE SINGLE-CHILD GENERATION

China's massive social experiment that created an entire generation of single children coincided with its rejection of socialist economics in favor of market-driven reforms. The expanded market now enables individuals to pursue personal goals and other opportunities independent of official approval. The new economic opportunities provide a mobility that was unimaginable in the Maoist era. Along with the government's rejection of the command economy was its decision to allow individuals more space in their personal lives. Divorce became easier, as did the opportunities to have affairs or casual sexual encounters. The opening of China as a vibrant economic and cultural setting coincided, particularly in the 1990s, with the entrance of the first generation of single children into their college years.

The Chinese often refer to contemporary youth as members of the post-1980 generation and the post-1990 generation, or *balinghou* and *jiulinghou*, respectively. These "generations" are conceived in terms of the decades within which they were born—the 1980s and the 1990s— and together they correspond, roughly, to the cohort referred to as "millennials" in Western literature. The *balinghou* and *jiulinghou* (also known as *bashihou* and *jiushihou*) are sometimes distinguished from each other in Chinese popular discourse, with the latter viewed as more individualistic and experimental than the former. These are distinctions that we need not belabor here.

The Chinese economy, feeling the effects of market reform, began to experience dramatic growth in the mid-1990s. Added to the economic opportunities brought about by this growth was the sudden access that young Chinese had to the Internet, also starting in the middle of that decade. Of course, Internet use was not restricted to the younger generation, but, as in Western countries, the young were the ones who used it most enthusiastically and skillfully.

As young Chinese were gaining access to international youth cultures, they were at the same time forging a national youth culture at home. The emergence of widespread Internet access was correlated with a new youth-controlled discourse with a shared vocabulary recognizable in every province of China. For example, the language of the new youth culture began to include references to "rights" and "freedom," as well as a number of youth-oriented slang expressions indicative of an emerging national youth culture. Prominent among these was the expression *"ku"* (or cool) with its individualistic connotations. In addition to *ku*, there were such written Internet terms as "mm" for *"meimei"* meaning "little sister," or, in youth slang discourse, "cute girl," and the numbers "88" for good-bye. The Mandarin pronunciation of "88" is *baba*, and the similarity of this expression to English "bye-bye" made this slangy usage at once both clever and cosmopolitan (Moore et al. 2010).

What particularly defines young Chinese today are the experiences they face as they have come of age in the Reform Era, experiences that made their lives fundamentally different from the lives of their parents. Their parents matured under the authority of a very intrusive Maoist state in the 1950s, 1960s and early 1970s. Under Maoism, their parents were, in their youth, expected to dedicate their lives to building a socialist society, and any attempts to promote their individual careers invited criticism or punishment from local authorities. Collectivism was a watchword of that era, as were devotion to Chairman Mao and suspicion of things foreign. The lives of Maoist-era urban youth were particularly closely controlled by the work unit or *danwei* to which each family was assigned. This meant that a young person's educational goals, leisure activities, and romantic relationships had to meet the approval of parents as well as the party leaders in the *danwei*. Rural life was similarly overseen by Communist Party administrators. Because of this tight control, the global youth culture that had been roiling much of the Western world since the 1960s had no effect on young Chinese before the beginning of the Reform Era. Chinese society was essentially a closed hierarchy where individual effort or achievement did not result in personal success. During this era, youth and their parents often referred to life as boring or meaningless (Jankowiak 2004). When Deng Xiaoping began to promote the economic reforms and the broad opening of society that eventually came to define the post-1978 years in China, the effects on Chinese families were immediate and ultimately quite dramatic. Three of the most significant effects were the encouragement of profit-oriented enterprise, the influx of global influences, and a pattern of sustained economic growth that lifted hundreds of millions of Chinese households to unprecedented levels of prosperity. Other factors that came into play at this time and contributed to the transformation of Chinese society were the institution of the one-child policy, the popularization of the Internet, and the gradual weakening of the *hukou* system (Chan and Buckingham 2008).

The *hukou* system of household registration was established in the 1950s "as a means of monitoring and controlling population mobility between countryside and the cities. All citizens were assigned at birth either rural or urban hukou status and generally were eligible for only the welfare and social services provided in their hometowns" (Mason 2016:39). The relaxing of the *hukou* system in the Reform Era contributed to the mobility of Chinese society domestically, just as the new policies of openness to the outside world created new opportunities for interaction with the international community. Although local governments continue to modify the law, the urban *hukou* does continue to be difficult to obtain, with the result that there is more suffering for migrants who have less access to relevant social services. Migrant laborers who live full time in the city without an urban *hukou* continued to be marginalized as second-class citizens. But for most Chinese, the weakening of the *hukou* system has been a plus, and more and more families are finding themselves in a position to reap the economic rewards that the Reform Era offers.

The changes ushered in by the Reform Era have had lasting impacts on Chinese families. Many that were only able to scrape by on modest incomes in 1980 were, by 1995, furnishing their homes with washing machines, color televisions, sophisticated stereo systems, and other previously unattainable consumer products. Along with these improved economic circumstances came changes in the values and attitudes of the children who grew up in the new prosperity. For many, the middle-class culture in which they reached adolescence seemed so normal and natural that the poverty and confined lives of their parents' youth were difficult to comprehend. China's urban millennials live in a world that is distinct from that of their parents' adolescence, not only materially but culturally and psychologically as well. These young Chinese are all about two things: self-fulfillment and positive affect—the very things that were anathema in the Maoist era. At the same time they also want to keep close ties with their parents.

The new social milieu of post-Reform adolescents is sometimes referred to as a "risk society," in which restrictions on one's life are reduced but the safety nets of the past are also gone. In this milieu, individual striving and expressiveness, once suppressed, were suddenly being embraced. One index of the millennial youths' individualism was the emergence of the above-mentioned slang expression "*ku*" in the 1990s. This term, derived from the global youth culture word "cool," was linked to individualism. Flamboyant rock stars as well as hyper-masculine heroes played by action stars like Chow Yun-fat and Jackie Chan were some of its exemplars (Moore 2005, Louie 2000).

The millennial youth of the People's Republic faced a world that differed from Hong Kong and Taiwan. These polities were never as tightly controlled as the PRC. Nor were they as isolated from international youth cultures. Thus, the Hong Kongese and Taiwanese youth never had to deal with the kind of generational divide faced by the millennials of the PRC. Though both Hong Kong and Taiwan experienced economic surges, these surges came earlier than they did in the PRC and were not instigated by dramatic reversals in government policy. Neither Hong Kong nor Taiwan went through periods of collectivism when individual striving was systematically suppressed.

That Taiwan saw an individualistic youth culture emerge long before the PRC did is illustrated in a study of young Taiwanese by Thomas Shaw (1994). According to Shaw, in Taiwan's capital city (Taibei), young middle-class Chinese in the 1980s were participating in a youth culture in which the dominant guiding principle was having fun. These Taiwanese adolescents, known as *kah-a*, pursued amusements in shopping malls, fast food restaurants, and discos, much as Western youth did. Their interest in music, dancing, and fashionable clothing also indicated that they were part of the global youth culture in a way that their contemporaries on the mainland were not. And the adolescents of Hong Kong, with even greater access to Western sources of popular culture than the Taiwanese, were similarly pursuing interests that paralleled those of young people in the West. But the difference in lifestyle between the young people of Hong Kong and Taiwan as opposed to that of mainland youth began to fade once the Reform Era was underway in the PRC. The openness, individualism, and style consciousness of young millennials in the PRC marked a major cultural shift away from the *danwei*-dominated Mao era. The stark cultural shift experienced by China's millennials contributed to a sense on the part of their elders that their children were growing up in a world they had trouble comprehending.

In modern societies younger generations are typically among the first promulgators of social change, and this has often been the case in China. But in China, the modern tendency for young people to introduce change often clashes with the Confucian ideal encouraging deference to parents. The conflict between youthful progressivism and traditional conservatism has at times dominated China's national discourse. As indicated in Chapter 4 for example, one of the most influential literary works of the twentieth century was Ba Jin's *Family*, a fictional account of the intergenerational struggle between a group of youthful brothers and their family patriarch over the right to select one's own spouse.

EMERGING ADULTHOOD

A significant shift for young Chinese brought about by Deng Xiaoping's reforms is the appearance of "emerging adulthood" (Arnett 2014; Jankowiak et al. 2012). Emerging adults are people of roughly eighteen to twenty-five years of age who don't regard themselves as fully adults but rather as being on the cusp of adulthood. Arnett's emerging adult category parallels what Yunxiang Yan refers to as "youth" among rural Chinese of Heilongjiang—those of about sixteen to twenty-five whose values are distinct from those of their elders (Yan 1999). What distinguishes emerging adults from those who are wholly adults is their having not quite reached a point in their lives where they can claim economic self-sufficiency nor a capacity to make independent decisions about how to organize their lives. Arnett's criteria for defining full adulthood is different from the tradition that regarded marriage and parenthood as adulthood's primary indicators. Actually most young people in the early decades of the PRC did not marry until they were well into their twenties, so it isn't late marriage per se that has given birth to emerging adulthood in China. Rather it is the possibilities offered by the new prosperity. The new distinguishing features of emerging adulthood in China are the focus on experimentation and on the establishing of an individual identity. Since the 1990s many young people have been living apart from their parents, enjoying employment in well-paying professional or commercial positions, and have thereby found the space to focus on personal issues that will ultimately shape their sense of who they are. This extended period of identity seeking, a prime feature of emerging adulthood in the West, corresponds with the rise of individualism among China's youth. But before such a life phase can appear in any society, there must be a level of prosperity characteristic of a middle class and a pattern of extended post-secondary education available to large numbers of youth. These qualities now characterize much of China, especially urban China, and they have made something of an appearance in rural China as well.

The social transformations of China's Reform Era can be seen as a third wave of modernization. The first two waves accompanied the reforms of the May Fourth Movement, and then the establishment of the PRC in 1949. Each of these first two transformations entailed new ways of thinking about society and the individual, and each was driven by intellectual or political leaders who were aiming at specific goals, such as the establishment of democracy or socialism. The changes brought about by Deng Xiaoping's reforms are best seen as unintended and unforeseen consequences. Deng's primary goal was prosperity for China; his aims did not include the appearance of a life phase in which young people spend several years as unmarried individuals whose primary focus was on determining what they would make of their lives. The new, gradually emerging image of the proper family ideal is still a work in progress. However, we can already see some significant trends: a parenting philosophy and practice designed to create a more independent or flexible self, capable of interacting in a variety of social contexts; and a heightened value for the pursuit of satisfying life goals.

As Fong (2004) has noted, PRC policy in the 1990s promoted education as a way to create a generation of youth with "high quality" (*gao suzhi rencai*). These increasingly available opportunities for education allowed many millennials to think not merely in terms of enhanced earning power but also of self-fulfillment. But this desire and its attendant pursuit of self-development often clashes with parental anxiety over performance in school. This tension is captured in one youth's comment:

> It's not fair that American students can spend so much time on leisure and still be successful....I wish China were like that. Then we'd be happier, and cultivate our abilities by listening to music, watching TV,

and playing around with friends, rather than spending so much time studying useless things in school. (Fong 2004: 176)

This young man, in addition to his frustration with the heavy emphasis on rote memorizing in Chinese schools, was also longing for an opportunity to pursue interests and develop his capacities in a way that would enable him to construct a satisfying identity. The longing he expresses would not and could not have been voiced by his parents in the 1960s or 1970s.

The interest in self-fulfillment is not confined to middle-class youth like those described in Fong's ethnography. Leslie Chang, writing about young migrant women in Guangdong Province, emphasizes that these migrants leave their rural homes not merely to boost their incomes but even more to broaden their experiences. In fact, Chang was surprised at how focused these migrant workers were on widening their horizons and experiencing urban life. One young woman explained her motivation for leaving her rural home thus: "I wanted to get out early, learn some things and see the world" (Chang 2009:10). Such explanations were typical of many of the women interviewed by Chang. Similarly, migrants from rural areas in Hohhot reported that among the reasons for their wanting to live in the city were those that allowed them to develop themselves by facing challenging circumstances (*duanlian ziji*), "to open their eyes" (*kaikuo yanjin*), and "to change themselves" (*gaibian ziji*).

Emotional or affective factors, beyond the traditional ones of devotion to parents and to the ideals of Confucian duty, are prominent characteristics of adolescents and emerging adults in China today. Being able to pursue individual interests or otherwise act as one pleases may have been a luxury in the past, but young Chinese now see these as valid goals. This new emphasis on affect as a source of motivation plays an important part in the way families are constructed. Being devoted to parents and looking to their welfare is often cast not in terms of duty but as a matter of affection (Sun 2013). Though statements of deep affection for parents were common enough in traditional China, today the emphasis (as discussed in Chapter 6) on affectionate ties may trump notions of tradition or duty. This does not mean parent-youth relationships are less important. China's youth are caught between dueling moral systems: one highlights duty and obligations, another emphasizes the freedom to pursue self-interest and the fulfillment of desires.

DATING AND SELF-DEVELOPMENT

The rise of affect as an important element in the family is particularly relevant to dating, marriage, and future husband-wife relations (Jankowiak and Li 2016). A dating culture implies that emotional involvement with a dating partner may or may not be long-term. There are, as a consequence, increasing expectations, anxieties, and reservations when young people think about whether they should remain involved. To this end, the restlessness that has become characteristic of contemporary Chinese life is most acutely experienced within an emergent youth phase that is filled with happiness, joy, and contentment as well as disappointment, regret, and anger over the difficulty and frustration associated with trying to find and hold on to a lover (Jankowiak 2013:211).

In the early years of the Reform Era (1980s), dating as a casual context within which young people could seek amusements together was unknown (Whyte and Parish 1984; Honig and Hershatter 1988). At that time, the powerful emotions associated with romantic involvement were sometimes discussed in official publications, and young people were routinely admonished to behave with both candor and restraint in their liaisons. In 1981 a young man reported in an issue of the *China Youth Daily* that he had courted six women in succession because he felt he needed to experiment before settling on a particular mate. Not surprisingly, given the spirit of that era, he was rebuked for this. In the 1980s young people were encouraged to take romantic affairs seriously as avenues to marriage, not as arenas for experimentation or pure fun (Jankowiak 1993, Honig and Hershatter 1988). But by the mid-1990s, as attitudes shifted, an entertainment-based dating culture took hold. Urban Chinese by this time were spending some of their evenings at dance halls, karaoke parlors, and other venues where many couples enjoyed themselves and only occasionally thought in terms of seeking a future spouse. The pursuit of leisure within and outside of a dating context, especially when it involves physical or educational adventures, is an avenue to self-development.

RURAL PATTERNS

Yan notes a somewhat similar pattern in a rural context: Heilongjiang in northeastern China. He identifies the conjugal family as the successor to the patriarchal extended family. This process of succession was gradual, beginning in 1950 and lasting until the end of the twentieth century. The key features of the conjugal family are the affection of husband and wife for each other, often openly expressed, and the shift in power toward the younger generation, partly on the basis of the strong marital bond. In fact, Yan identifies "the rise of conjugality" as one of the most significant social changes of the late twentieth century in rural China (2003:87). The conjugal families described by Yan in the 1990s displaced numerous patriarchal structures that had managed to endure through the Maoist era despite the Communist Party's egalitarian principles. Conjugal families and the individualism underlying them were in part enabled by the collective's individualistic work point system, mass schooling, legally enforced freedom in mate choice, job opportunities outside the agricultural sector, and new patterns of property transfer between generations (Yan 1999, 2003).

Yan describes, for example, one particularly feisty bride who resisted her widowed father-in-law when he tried to bully her. As was the custom, he had moved in with his newly married son, the younger of two brothers. He had reportedly been short-tempered and domineering all his adult life, and was known to have repeatedly beaten his (now deceased) wife. But his new daughter-in-law was not about to let him dominate her. She insisted on her right and that of her husband to manage the household. At one point she angrily confronted her father-in-law with these defiant words:

> I know you treated my mother[in-law] like a hired maid and you beat her as often as you ate your meals. What kind of a person are you! Don't ever think you can play the tyrant at home any more. Let me tell you, I am a capable person with a middle-school education. I was sent to this family by the ghost of my mother-in-law to fight you. (Yan 1999)

The continuing endurance of elements associated with the patriarchal family is a feature that distinguishes rural communities from urban ones. In Yan's village, traditional patriarchies had to be undone before the individualism and conjugality of contemporary China could take hold. But in urban China, starting with the 1919 May Fourth Movement and intensifying with China's Communist revolutionary reforms, patriarchy was relentlessly criticized and gradually dismantled. In the process the family lost most of its economic, political, and social resources, which resulted in the diminishing of parental authority (Parish and Whyte 1978).

The dismantling of the *danwei* combined with the development of a vibrant "market economy" provided youth with the public zones within which to meet and socialize. Unlike in most North American communities, these public zones were also occupied by adults. In this way, Chinese society, much like European societies, does not raise its youth as a "tribe apart" (Schlegel 1983). Consequently, until the massive migration of adults into the city which left offspring alone and thus incompletely socialized, Chinese youth were less likely than their American counterparts to engage in such problematic or dangerous behavior as drug use or binge drinking.

BOREDOM IN THE PRE-REFORM ERA / NEW YOUTH CULTURE ENTERTAINMENTS

Student life, before the economic and communicative forces of the Reform Era were felt, tended to be somewhat dull. University students complained about the bland and low-quality food offered in school cafeterias, and when they had some pocket money, they would typically spend it on meals at local restaurants. Also, when returning from visits home, they often waxed eloquent over the delicious meals they had enjoyed there.

Before the opening of video game parlors, discotheques, and karaoke parlors, all of which began to appear in virtually every Chinese city during the 1990s, male students spent much of their leisure time playing cards or eating out at restaurants. Female students were less inclined to play card games, but spent much of their leisure time taking walks and chatting with their roommates and friends. But sources of fun and entertainment were not as abundant as they later came to be in China.

It was also in the late 1980s and the 1990s when rock groups like Hei Bao and Tang Dynasty grew popular. It has become increasingly common for youth to attend rock concerts and to appreciate the messages of popular musicians. For example, in *Like a Knife* (1992), Andrew Jones describes the growing significance of rock music and its attendant ideology for contemporary Chinese young people. Cui Jian, sometimes referred to as China's Bob Dylan, is extremely well known and appreciated. Many of the single-child generation parents fondly recall his performance in Tiananmen Square during the 1989 protests.

The influence of global youth cultures can be seen in the transformations that some young style-conscious Chinese exhibited in the 1990s. Kicking Bird, a strikingly rebellious student at Qingdao University in the mid-1990s, stands as one example of this trend. Kicking Bird took his name from a Native American character he admired in the film *Dances with Wolves*. In addition to adopting a Native American name, young Kicking Bird also let his hair grow, Sioux Indian style, to a length well below his shoulders. This was at a time when the only other Chinese sporting such long hair were to be found in major cities like Beijing and Shanghai, not in secondary cities like Qingdao. His appearance was so striking that the university authorities decided that he had to leave school. But, with the support of his mother, Kicking Bird managed to maintain his place as a Qingdao University student. He even gained a bit of prestige among his classmates for his successful protest against the conservative dress and grooming codes of the school. As an individualistic, style-conscious young man, influenced by Western media and defiant toward local authorities, Kicking Bird in many ways represented the emerging youth culture value of "cool" (*ku*). However, his winning card turned out to be the support his mother offered him in his fight with the university. In other words, Kicking Bird expressed his individualistic flair within the framework of a family system that validated intense parental involvement in the lives of young adults (Moore and Rizor 2008). Chinese adolescents and emerging adults since the 1990s can be said in general to represent a kind of blending of these two currents, the new, globally influenced, style-conscious individualism, side by side with a family-based reciprocal support system including parents who see their children as the basis of their own futures (Fong 2004). The existence of dual moral systems is not necessarily always empowering. It may have contributed in part to the increase in the frequency of mental illness among China's youth. The Ministry of Health estimates 15 percent of Chinese youth have mental problems, and 30 million youth suffer from depression (Li et al. 2008: 397).

YOUTH AND FAMILY HARMONY IDEAL

Chinese trends since the 1990s illustrate that even when a younger generation initiates change, this does not necessarily result in the sudden appearance of social values and behaviors that have no connection with tradition. One well-entrenched ideal that continues to hold sway in a number of Chinese contexts is that of harmony, a value that has a deep genealogy in China. As Dien, for example, has noted, the preferred Chinese "mode of resolving conflict is reconciliation" (1982:335). And the ideal of family harmony as an important factor in parent-adolescent relations was made evident in a questionnaire survey addressing, among other things, intergenerational conflict. In 1994 Moore distributed questionnaires to 231 undergraduates at Tsinghua University, Qingdao University, Beijing Aerospace University, and Luoyang Teachers College. Three of the questions were specifically aimed at determining the age at which adolescents had had their most serious dispute with their parents, what the dispute was about, and how it was resolved. The most typical age range of adolescents experiencing such disputes was from fourteen to seventeen. China was just beginning to enjoy real prosperity, and young people were gaining access to the Internet and other avenues connecting them to the global youth culture. Though the values purveyed in rock music, Western films, and television programs might lead one to believe that young Chinese would begin to exhibit a pronounced rebellious streak, this turned out not to be the case. In fact, only 48 percent of the respondents (111) reported having had serious disputes with their parents during their adolescence. This contrasts with a rate of 82 percent of a sample of 240 American university students who were asked the same questions (Moore 2015).

For these young Chinese, the most common sources of conflict were romantic relationships or not studying enough. These two issues are actually related, in that parents often declared that their children shouldn't waste any time on romantic affairs because such behavior would undermine their ability to do well in school. In particular, the demands of the dreaded National College Entrance Exam (*gaokao*) requires that students spend much of their after-school time studying. This exam is taken around graduation time by every student who hopes to pursue postsecondary education. For many a high school graduate it will represent a life-shaping turning point, since it will determine the postsecondary education to which he or she will have access. Parents are keenly aware of the exam's significance, and in many families one or both parents will dedicate a great deal of time and energy encouraging their offspring to study long and hard. The importance of this exam, and the need for students to spend endless hours memorizing information and developing math skills in order to do well on it, means that many of the households in which adolescents lived were prone to tension as parents pushed their students to work ever harder, and students responded to the rapidly growing temptations offered by youth-oriented entertainments and, particularly, the allure of romantic attachments.

A third issue revealed by the questionnaires was the universities to which students wanted to submit applications. Choosing the right school is a significant decision that involves a degree of guesswork. A Chinese university will admit students only if their *gaokao* score meets a particular specified minimum. Different universities, depending on their prestige and exclusiveness, will have different minimum standards. Ordinarily a student will enter the most prestigious university that his or her *gaokao* score will allow, but applications are sent before the test is taken. This means that trying to estimate what one's score will be—and therefore to what schools one might reasonably submit *gaokao* scores and applications—is a guessing game. Parents often urge their offspring to apply to specific universities and even to select a specific major. Most students simply accept their parents' recommendation and apply to schools and programs accordingly, but some resist.

The widespread acceptance of parental advice on where to attend and what to major in is in part a reflection of the deeply ensconced cultural idea that parents know what is best for their children. Several questionnaire responses specifically alluded to the inherently superior wisdom of parents as explanations for their deferring to their parents' position. The traditional ideal of filial piety reinforces this. These two factors, along with intense parental interest in their offspring's long-term prospects, result in many Chinese assuming that parents will involve themselves closely in both career-shaping decisions and in romantic and marriage-related decisions as well. In this new milieu, parents' authority should be weakened. Jankowiak and Li (2016) found, however, that unlike the 1980s, where urban offspring ignored parental mate selection urgings, the single-child generation, especially daughters, are particularly influenced by a mother's opinion.

Some problems associated with global youth cultures are not especially prominent in China. Neither drug nor alcohol use were indicated as sources of problems by our questionnaire respondents. Drugs are not as widespread in China as they are in many Western countries, though their use is on the increase (Khan et al. 2014). Drug use is much more prominent in noncollege or working-class youth than among students. Alcohol is widely consumed, but its consumption by adolescents is not regarded as a problem. Social drinking is seen as normal behavior, and many Chinese families include their adolescent offspring when beer, *baijiu*, or other alcoholic beverages are served at the family table.

When serious disputes did arise, the respondents reported relying on discussion with the hope of compromise as their most typical coping strategy. Fourteen of the respondents in our sample (13 percent) reported that their dispute was settled through compromise. In the absence of compromise, one side almost always succeeded in resolving the dispute through persuasion. More often than not, it was the adolescent who persuaded the parent (Moore 2015).

A number of students specified that the settlement was reached for the sake of the greater entity, that is, the family. In this way, family harmony was maintained in all three of the most common dispute-settlement results: adolescent victory, parental victory, and compromise. In fact, these three kinds of outcomes account for almost three-quarters of all disputes among the Chinese respondents. American students, when asked similar questions, are much more likely than their Chinese counterparts to report an ongoing guerrilla war against their parents, or a peaceful relationship established through the adolescent deceiving parents as to the nature of his or her behavior (Moore 2015).

The notion of a "cold war" did, however, appear in a few Chinese questionnaires. One female student reported that a dispute about her failure to study diligently resulted in "one and a half years of cold war, then mutual forgiving." Another female described herself as being close to a boy she liked at the age of fourteen. Her parents objected strenuously and the result was "cold war to the end." These "cold war" references represent exceptions to the rule that says members of a family should seek harmony above all. They are a minor exception, however, given that there were only three such references in all 111 disputes.

A distinguishing trend of millennial Chinese revealed in the questionnaire responses that appears to be a consequence of access to global youth cultures is the tendency to use language reflecting a belief in young people's "rights." A Beijing Aerospace student said, for example, that her most serious adolescent conflict with her parents was due to their forbidding her to do something she liked to do. In her words, they "interfered with my freedom." A young man from the same university talked about his "right" to stay out all night, and one Tsinghua University male student said conflict arose because he "challenged parental authority." Phrases referencing such concepts as "freedom," "rights," and "challenges to parental authority" represent a new kind of language for young Chinese. Our questionnaires, then, reveal a continuation of traditional values, particularly the emphasis on family harmony, but they also illustrate some emerging trends engendered by the rise of individualism among millennial Chinese.

GENDER RELATIONSHIPS

The changes that have come about as the millennial generation has shifted to a more individualistic and affect-driven ethos has shaken up not only parent-child relationships but gender relationships as well. Young females have benefited from the one-child policy and the rise of individualism; they have improved status and expanded opportunities. The one-child policy means, for many families, that their "only hope" for a secure future lies not only with a son but also with a daughter (Fong 2004, Jankowiak 2013). Lihong Shi (2011) found a similar trend—and sometimes a preference for daughters—in northern Chinese villages. With the shift away from farming to manufacturing and service work, there is no need for a son to remain behind and work the family farm. Moreover, the skewed sex ratio has enabled women to demand an ever more costly bride price. Taken together, many families are reevaluating the historical preference for sons in favor of daughters.

The prized place that daughters now enjoy in their families is further enhanced by the widespread belief that women are better caretakers of elderly parents than are men. Thus, many parents of singleton girls regard a daughter as particularly worthy of both affection and trust as a potential future caregiver. Even the status of daughter-in-law, once the lowliest position in the patriarchal family, has taken on a new luster in light of the rising hopes that families now place on the women of the millennial generation (Santos 2016, Engebretsen 2016). In some families, the mother-daughter bond has replaced the father-son bond as the backbone of intergenerational solidarity. An incident observed by Fong in one of her informants' households illustrates this dynamic. The parents of teenage daughter Chen Nan are arguing (and occasionally pleading their respective cases to the ethnographer) over which of them should cook dinner, the ailing mother or the just-home-from-work father.

"Why don't you cook dinner for once, Pa?" Chen Nan interjected. "Ma isn't feeling well. Let her rest. She does all the work around here. Can't you let her rest for once?"

"My daughter takes her Ma's side, as always!" Chen Nan's father complained to me. "Why can't she take my side for once?"

"She's not taking my side. She's just being fair," Chen Nan's mother said smugly from the bed where she still lay.

"You think she's good to you now, but wait till she marries," Chen Nan's father snapped at his wife. "A daughter is water spilled on the ground. Once she's married, she'll forget all about us."

"That's not true!" Chen Nan protested. "I'll be filial even after I'm married, just like Ma is to Grandma!"

"That's what you say now, but I know what you'll do once you marry out!" Chen Nan's father replied.

"Well then, I'll never marry! I'll stay with Ma forever!" Chen Nan said. Then, with a mischievous grin at her mother, she added, "But we'll have to kick Pa out." (Fong 2004:153)

This scenario reveals not only the warmth between mother and daughter and the daughter's declaration of filiality, but also the father's recourse to a traditional patrilineal principle, one quite thoroughly abandoned in today's urban families: the idea that a daughter will be like water spilled onto the earth once she marries: unrecoverable.

Young urban women are advantaged in that they do not face one of the heavier pressures felt by young men: the expectation that the man should provide housing for a newly married couple. In previous decades the *danwei* provided housing, but as this is no longer the case, this expectation for emerging adult males is among the most challenging they will face. Along with this is the fact that the one-child policy and the increase in educational opportunities in reform China have resulted in competition for employment with women. For well-educated urbanites, this is usually not a serious problem, since men and women both are likely to find employment. But for those with little or no secondary education, prospects for jobs in the service economy are actually better for women than for men, resulting in the marginalization of some youth (Jankowiak et al. 2012).

In rural areas, the factors underlying changes in gender relationships overlap with those found in urban areas, but do not match them exactly. For one thing, male births outnumber female births in China by a ratio of about 120 to 100 (Greenhalgh 2013), and this gender imbalance is much more pronounced in rural areas than in urban ones. The imbalance reflects historic parental preferences for sons over daughters, a traditional mindset that has all but vanished in the urban middle class and is finally beginning to disappear among China's rural families as well (Shi 2017). In the face of official pressures to restrict family size, the birth of one or more daughters has been interpreted by some rural parents as a threat to their future well-being, and this has resulted in the widespread aborting of female fetuses, the neglect of daughters, and the abandonment of newborns. The resulting gender imbalance, itself a consequence of traditional male favoritism, places a measure of bargaining power into the hands of marriageable adult women. Young men, particularly in more impoverished rural areas, may simply never find a suitable mate willing to marry them. These "involuntary bachelors" suffer not only from the difficulties inherent in their unmarried status, but even further due to public discourse that all too often assumes them to be sources of trouble (Greenhalgh 2013).

Other advantages enjoyed by young rural women include their relative mobility. This mobility comes partly from the household registry system, which accepts the traditional assumption that a new bride will move into her husband's home at marriage. Women also generally find it easy to migrate to urban sites where they readily find work, given that many factory bosses prefer female employees to males, and a number of service occupations are also considered more suitable for female employees (Chang 2009).

Female mobility and extra leverage in marriage prospects are supplemented by the control that newly married young women have over family property, a Reform-Era development in rural family relations. The juxtaposition of women's power, if not authority, in terms of bride wealth negotiation, size of dowry, and property holding is historic and signals the end of Chinese patriarchy and the rise of the woman as the central force in the conjugal family. These new patterns have engendered what Yan refers to as "girl power" in rural China (Yan 2009). According to Yan, girl power is often at bottom an expression of youth power: young women, with the support of their husbands, pushing against the traditional strictures that used to make life so difficult for Chinese daughters-in-law. In light of this, Yan distinguishes the undermining of the patriarchy in rural China, which is based on greater power being in the hands of young women, with a generalized androcentrism, or favoritism for males that lives on in extra-familial contexts (Yan 2003). The male centrism identified by Yan parallels the male favoritism illustrated by Osburg in his study of network building among wealthy urbanites (Osburg 2013). Osburg's study focused primarily on wealthy rural men who had established successful businesses in the city of Chengdu. They continued to embrace rural values and understandings of what is and is not a proper family. Moreover, their pursuit of self-development and personal autonomy was tempered by a commitment to maintain strong interdependent social bonds. This is less critical for urban youth, who prefer a more egalitarian intergenerational relationship along with more intimate, and thus personal, parent-child bonding that allows for the expression of the self and private feelings (Sun 2013). In gender relationships among Chinese millennials, as with so many other factors affecting the modern family, diversity—urban vs. rural, regional, and so forth—must be kept in mind.

Conclusion: Intergenerational Exceptions and Uncertainties

My great love is to my grandmother—she is the most special person. I love to visit her and wash her feet. It makes her feel good because she knows I love her so much.

> (A nineteen-year-old college student, from William Jankowiak's unpublished field notes)

If you want to be remembered have a daughter. Daughters will never forget you.

> (A fifty-eight-year-old urban woman, from William Jankowiak's unpublished field notes)

The Chinese family in the twentieth and early twenty-first century has undergone a series of changes, some quite sudden and dramatic and others more gradual and nuanced. These changes themselves did not have uniform effects on every Chinese community, and the consequence of these changes and their varying permutations is a wide array of family systems, ranging from those of the urbanized coastal areas to those more typical of the landlocked interior. Even within this urban-rural divide there is as much diversity as there is uniformity. Particularly notable in terms of their distinct differences are many of the minority communities in such territories as Tibet and western Yunnan as mentioned in Chapter Three.

In very broad terms, we can say that Han China entered the twentieth century embedded in a longstanding and ongoing Confucian tradition that emphasized deference to parents and elders, favoritism for males, and an understanding of inheritance, both material and conceptual, that was strongly patrilineal. These attributes underlie most popular views of the Chinese family. And at its core the Chinese family was anchored in a moral system that stressed that individuals in the junior generations were obligated to assist and care for their elders.

Exposure to powerful global influences, particularly those of relatively liberal Western societies, had begun to provoke questions about this tradition by the turn of the twentieth century. But the tradition nevertheless remained dominant during the waning days of the Qing dynasty. The dramatic upheaval of the May Fourth Movement in 1919 and the subsequent flood of new ideas about science, democracy, and individual rights shattered this unitary Confucian ideal, though it did not sweep away all of its effects. Many Han Chinese, particularly in rural areas where the impact of the post-1919 New Culture Movement was relatively weak, continued to see the family as an essentially patrilineal and patriarchal entity, and one whose hierarchical structure gave moral and material authority to elders.

Marxist ideals, which also gained some prominence during the post-May Fourth upheaval, added a powerfully egalitarian thrust to ideas about what a proper Chinese family should look like. The Chinese Communist Party was founded just two years after May 4, 1919, and soon made its influence felt both in urban centers and in "liberated" rural districts. The victory of the CCP in 1949 meant that Marxist ideals would soon have an impact in every corner of the People's Republic of China, even in such non-Han areas as Tibet and Xinjiang. One of the most powerful instruments of Marxist thinking came in the form of the Marriage Law of 1950, which explicitly outlawed arranged marriages and insisted on equality for females, at least where rights of inheritance were concerned.

After the establishment of the People's Republic in 1949, and before the beginning of the Reform Era, the Chinese family confronted a series of shocks mainly resulting from an effort by Communist Party leaders to obliterate the kin-based power structures of the old Confucian clans and families. One consequence of this was the empowering of young people; a further inadvertent consequence was increased individualism. The Marriage Law of 1950 contributed to this trend by insisting that marriages should be based on free choice as well as on love. In other words, marriages, which had for centuries reflected parental ideas about control of property and maintenance of the kin group, were now to be fundamentally individualistic and affect-driven.

This individualistic/affective complex took off in a dramatic way after 1980, once the forces of the market and the influences of global youth cultures hit the People's Republic. Adding to these new forces was the one-child policy, established in 1979 and maintained with varying success in different communities until 2015. This policy resulted in a generation of singletons, especially in urban China, whose parents looked to them as the very embodiment of the future (Fong 2004). This role thrust these young millennials into a contradictory status: they were newly empowered as individuals but at the same time burdened by the sense that they represented the future to their parents.

A further consequence of the one-child policy was the sudden growth of an imbalance in the gender ratio of the millennial generation, as millions of families used abortions and other techniques to ensure sons rather than daughters. The 30 million or so young millennial men who face the prospect of failing to find a wife due to the lack of women in their generation present a major problem for China as a whole. It also forces the families of young men who have almost no marriage prospects to face a situation that they consider deeply tragic: the likelihood that they will never marry and will not be able to carry on their family line. Women of this generation are, on the other hand, empowered in the marriage market: they are a scarce resource (Li and Hu, 2014). But other social and economic forces (including, for example, biases in some employment sectors) remain quasi-patriarchal and undermine female power, despite the advantages that the marriage arena offers women.

The power of family elders has been weakened by the redefinition of the family-household in such a way that it is no longer the primary production unit. The socialist state has redefined filial piety and in the popular imagination this value has come to be seen as emotionally valid where appropriate but not an absolute duty. Those who cling to filial piety as a duty are likely to be viewed as strikingly old-fashioned in their mentality. This change in the nature of filial piety, along with others, has undermined the elders' moral authority. Other factors have also steadily diminished the material leverage of the older generation as well as the political support they may have once enjoyed vis-à-vis recalcitrant offspring (Dos Santos 2008).

Increasingly, for many parents, the only "resource of power" left to them was the emotional bond they were able to forge with their off-spring. Where control of material resources is concerned, the response of offspring to their parents has come to be calculated largely in terms of the perceived need of the older generation (Chen et al. 2005). If their parents had adequate funds, their children made a token monetary contribution or, in some cases, gave nothing at all. But for parents who were not in a financially sound condition, particularly if they required substantial support, children typically tried to see to their needs as best they could. Martin Whyte found a similar pattern in his 1994 survey of the families of Baoding, a small northern city. In fact, he found no signs of a crisis of filial support.

Vanessa Fong (2004) found that among the Dalian parents she interviewed, there were some grounds for concern, partly because of governmentally mandated retirement. Because of China's relatively early retirement policies (age fifty-five for women and sixty for men), "the Chinese state practically guarantees that most [elderly spend their final days almost completely] dependent upon their children" (Fong 2004: 128). Such a situation, given the financial dependence it creates, can bring a serious level of insecurity to urban elders who, like their village counterparts, are ever more dependent on their children's support. In this way, China's enormous societal changes have profoundly affected intergenerational relationships.

FILIAL PIETY: HOW RELIABLE ARE EMOTIONAL TIES?

Filial obligations comprise two aspects: the obligation to obey your parents in all realms, and the obligation to support them in old age and be very attentive to their needs and desires. Traditionally the level of emotional intimacy was not crucial (Martin Whyte, email correspondence, April 2016). But the formal nature of filial piety has gradually been replaced by a more informal concept, one organized around affection and reciprocal considerations based on positive memories. The need for respect for and obedience to one's parents and the obligation to support them have lost much of their weight, though they are still present. Martin Whyte (1997) found that the intergenerational bond is organized around a reciprocal relationship that is for the most part affective, though it also entails material exchanges. This exchange includes the expectation that parents will pay for the education, marriage, and material wellbeing of their offspring, who will in turn care for them in their later years. Goh, in the southern city of Xiamen, however, showed that the sentiment on which care for one's elders is based cannot always be relied on. Many times, she reports, grandparents feel exploited and even humiliated. But, Goh points out, the only child is not a lone tactician who engages with caretakers in an effort to manipulate them (Goh 2006). A child, however, can be an astute "politician" in striving to get what he or she wants in the family context. The PRC government, recognizing that the newly emerging family form might leave elders vulnerable included in the 1950 marriage law a stipulation obligating children to see to their elders' needs. In fact, most Chinese felt an obligation to see to their parents' welfare even without being legally obligated to do so.

Yuezhu Sun (2013) found an enormous shift in the underlying motives invoked by young adult Beijing Chinese to explain their support for or commitment to their parents' wellbeing. Their explanations were not generally anchored in terms of simple or straightforward notions about ethics or responsibility. Increasingly single children now stress the development of an emotional connection as a critical factor in shaping the intensity of their commitment to their parents and the need to see to their parents' wellbeing. A typical illustration of this new and somewhat complex attitude can be seen in a female singleton who explained that she was happy and contented with her parents. She adds: "I think I am very lucky to have such parents. My father gives me the security a family provides. I went to a boarding school for high school; one day I felt very depressed and alone so I called my father. My father said to me that I missed home because I missed the people at home...he said he would never let me feel bad all by myself."

A similar example of an offspring's devotion is evident in a young man's recollection of his parents' love: "A lot of Chinese parents, including my parents, wish the best for their children. They get them into the best school; give them the best food, and best clothes. This is not doting or spoiling. This is not materialism. Not at all. This is parental love. They want the best for their children."

Still another youth fondly recalled her mother's love and care. When, as a child, she had suffered from smallpox, her mother applied medicine to her skin and comforted her, saying, "Dear baby, let mommy help you with medicine." She added, "I often told my parents I love them and it is good to have them....I truly enjoy the way we communicate with each other" (Sun 2013:5).

The strength of these memories is evident in that Sun found in every instance that the single child's commitment to his or her parents was anchored not so much in material exchange but in sentiment. This reference to affect as the driving force behind filiality challenges China's longstanding ethical code, a code that once declared that children owe obedience and support to their parents, regardless of the quality of their interpersonal relationship.

Recently voices have made an appearance in cyberspace arguing that children owe their parents nothing if those parents did not establish a warm, affectionate environment during their childhood. Xia Zhang's Chongqing-based investigation of cyber postings revealed a marginal group that called itself the "anti-parents clique." They argued for a redefinition of traditional morality where family obligations are concerned. They insisted that obligations should be based on warm affectionate bonds, and not on simple adherence to longstanding conventions. This, they maintained, is especially so when an individual's feelings for his or her parents are negative or virtually absent.

Rubie Watson has declared that "unconditional filial piety, which was based on the sacredness of parenthood, no longer exists" (Watson 2007:19). For both rural and urban youth, "intergenerational reciprocity has to be balanced and maintained through consistent exchange" (Watson 2007:19). And this exchange, even when symbolized through material goods or property, must be fundamentally expressive of positive sentiment.

Among urbanites in the PRC, the elderly prefer to live alone if they can manage to do so, rather than with their adult children (Whyte 2005:28). They hope and expect that their children will look after them if they become infirm, but they also want to live self-sufficient lives and so avoid being a burden to their children. Living alone also implies that they will retain some control over their lives. For example,

Shen's (2009) Shanghai investigation found that whenever parents move into their son's new house, they assume that the young couple is the host and they are guests who should defer to their son's and daughter-in-law's judgement. The power relationship in such a household is diametrically different from that found in a classical patriarchy. Shen observed that in every instance the young couple retained the larger master bedroom with the better view, while the parent(s) took the smaller bedroom. Significantly, everyone considers the house as belonging to the young couple, even if it was bought with their parents' money.

These preferred living arrangements are a sign that conjugal intimacy, which itself has come to be viewed as affective rather than duty-bound, now supersedes parental authority in most households. This is a drastic change. Certainly no observer of Chinese society in the early twentieth century would have envisioned a future in which elderly parents would prefer to live alone so as not to be a "burden" to their offspring, and in which intergenerational bonds would be tacitly redefined in terms of emotion rather than Confucian duties. A major consequence of these changes is that by 2000, nuclear families had become the new norm, accounting for over half the households in China (Wang 2012).

Different regions seem to be moving toward the nuclear-family household pattern at different rates. Charlotte Ikels, for example, reports that 60 percent of the elderly in the households she surveyed in Guangzhou (in southeastern China) included co-resident married offspring (Ikels 2004). But in Baoding, 100 miles southwest of Beijing, Whyte (1997) found that only 35 percent of parents over fifty lived with their married offspring. Myron Cohen (1998) working in a northern village found 72 percent of the families conjugal, with only 22 percent of parents living with their married adult children. Likewise Yan (2003) found that 30 percent of elders (over sixty years old) lived alone or with a spouse. As Li and Lamb point out, this trend is empowering for adults in the younger generation, allowing young parents to exert their authority independently of the senior generation's preferences (Li and Lamb 2013:22). Living separately does not, of course, mean that household cooperation between elders and married children ends. In fact, mutual support is the norm between parents and children as it is between adult siblings who live in separate households (Watson 2007).

Socialistic reforms were not the only factors bringing about change in twentieth-century China. Other Confucian societies in East Asia have undergone similar transformations in household composition without the intervention of Marxist administrators. Both Japan and South Korea offer evidence to this effect. For example, in "1981, 59 percent of Japanese elderly surveys choose to cohabit with their children, in 2001, the number decreased to 44 percent. For Korean elderly, the difference is even more dramatic. The percentage of Korean elderly who thought it was ideal to live with their children fell from 83 percent in 1981 to 34 percent in 2001" (Yang 2013:3).

Self-sacrifice for the family stands in "tension with the values associated with individualism, such as autonomy, mobility, and choice" (Liu 2008: 417). Alarmed by the increasing indifference toward helping one's parents among some young Chinese, the government instituted the "Protection of the Rights and Interests of Elderly People" law specifying that children have a legal and moral duty to attend to the material and spiritual needs of the elderly (Wong 2013). The government seemed to assume that elder care would naturally continue due to requirements of filial piety. It never considered the possibility that the rise of affective bonds or the demands of pragmatic considerations (such as children living and working in different cities) would pose a problem. Another hindrance to caring for elderly parents is the limited housing available to most young urbanites, who typically live in tiny, shoebox-like apartments that don't have room for three generations. Furthermore, given the limited number of children born to couples today, a single child may face economic and other difficulties in caring for elderly parents and possibly parents-in-law. While it may be the case that early socialist policies undermined the multigeneration family, it is certainly the case that the search for freedom and new wealth unleashed by the Reform Era finally and utterly dismembered China's traditional family structure (Economist 2015b:35).

But what is a problem for aging urbanites is an even more serious problem in rural areas. Rebecca Myerson et al. (2010) found that China's internal, rural-to-urban migration has had serious consequences for the ways in which migrants redefine their obligations toward their natal families. Migrants, while continuing to uphold the importance of filial piety, are, like their urban counterparts, rejecting blind adherence to traditional morality. They are also increasingly coming to value independence, mobility, and the right to redefine their lives in ways they find meaningful. In effect, personal agency has become an important value, not always to the benefit of the elders left behind.

Because rural villagers do not enjoy state-sponsored retirement pensions, they commonly rely on their own long-term strategies to ensure their old age security. For most, the best way to be sure that their children remember their filial obligations is to be generous toward them, relying on material gifts to express their affection. Supporting an adult son by paying for his wedding is a typical way in which parents show they are ready to step up on behalf of their children. Both affection and guilt may result from such generosity, as well as feelings of obligation on the part of the son to repay his parents for their support. Hong Zhang (2005) also found a similar strategy, in which parents invest greater resources and time with each child in hopes that their offspring will reciprocate. In some cases this may backfire, however. Yan's (2003) rural investigation revealed that this parental generosity strategy motivated some youth to be more aggressive about demanding a large bride price, which they would wind up keeping for themselves (2002: 650).

Another new feature of the rural family is the growing appreciation for daughters. Lihong Shi (2009:350), working in a northern village, discovered that the valuation of sons over daughters was changing toward a clear preference for daughters as the primary caretakers of parents in old age. Parents often repeated a popular Chinese folk saying: "A daughter is like a little quilted vest to warm her parents' hearts." The preference for daughters over sons is not based on conventional obligations, but rather, in stark contrast to tradition, arises out of pragmatic considerations as well as deep-seated emotional bonds forged in childhood. Shi also found that most married sons who lived in the same village as their parents did not visit them as frequently as did daughters who also lived in the village. Moreover, when sons did visit they did not express concern for their parents the way daughters routinely did. Many villagers were delightfully surprised that their married daughters would shoulder the responsibility to provide medical care and food provisions. Further, villagers told Shi that daughters helped with domestic chores and physical care more than their sons did. In the 1980s, Jankowiak (1993) found a similar gender bias in an urban environment: daughters more than sons took care of their natal parents. Ideas about appropriate gendered behavior seems to have played a part in these different ways of expressing affection. A number of men confided to Shi that they "wanted to show intimacy to their parents but felt shy about expressing their emotions for fear of leaving people with the impression that they were woman-like" (Shi 2009:363). Jankowiak found men voicing similar responses. Chinese men find that carrying out their obligations and responsibilities, when combined with performance of expected gender norms, can be more restrictive than it is for women.

According to Shi, unfilial behavior is much more likely to come from a son, or a son backed up by his wife, than it is from a daughter (2009:355). As one example of this phenomenon, she offers the tragic story of Chen and her husband, Hong. After marriage, the couple's son moved in with his parents, but it soon became clear that his wife could not get along with his mother. What started out as a minor conflict grew more intense one day when Chen did not open the gate quickly enough to let the cows in for the evening. An angry quarrel erupted and before long the young wife's mother came to the village to support her daughter. A physical fight broke out, in which Chen suffered a minor injury. Immediately the daughter-in-law demanded that the elderly couple move out from what had once been their own home. If Chen and her husband refused to move, she said she would divorce their son and keep the bride price and then go find someone else to marry. Given the large sex ratio imbalance, it would have been easy for the daughter-in-law to find a new husband. Their son, on the other hand, would have some difficulty finding a new wife, especially in the absence of a sizable bride price. To protect their son's interests, Chen and Hong moved out by 10:30 that evening (Shi 2009:355). This case is not unique. The lopsided sex ratio has turned women into a scarce resource, especially in rural communities. This gives them the leverage to make demands that would have been unthinkable before the Reform Era.

Shi offers another account of a young married woman, but this one is illustrative of the reciprocal bonds of affection that, for many contemporary Chinese, are taking the place of traditional notions of filial duty. In this case, an adopted daughter, Yulan, was given away as a child after her biological parents divorced. She grew deeply attached to her new parents and when she turned nineteen and started to work in the village health care store, she had income to bring home to them along with tasty treats and good clothes. Once she was married, she could have moved away to her husband's village, as most traditional brides did, but instead she talked her husband into staying in her village so she could take care of her parents. Her affective priorities were strikingly evident when, by coincidence, her adopted father died on the same day as her biological father. When funerals were held for both of these men, she attended her adopted father's ceremony and ignored that of her biological father. According to Shi, the villagers had high praise for Yulan's self-sacrifice and her dedication to her adoptive parents (Shi 2009:358). But Yulan's behavior, of course, was rooted in sentiment, in her emotional attachment to the adoptive parents who cared for her throughout her childhood. This case, alongside that of Chen and Hong's daughter-in-law, cited above, illustrate a nationwide transformation in which the patriarchal authority of the senior generation has been undermined, and a renegotiation of intergenerational relations is taking place (Shi 2009:359).

The changes that have transformed China since the beginning of the Reform Era have created problems along with opportunities. China now has the third highest elderly suicide rate in the world (Lee and Kleinman 2003). These authors found that in one region (Hunan) the leading cause of suicide was the despair brought on in the face of chronic disease (23.6 percent). But following close behind were a number of causes reflecting the shifting power relationships between generations. These included, for example, desertion by family members (20.3 percent), anger due to abuse by children (12.2 percent), and pessimism caused by an offspring's habitual gambling (9.4 percent) (cited in Watson 2007:16). Those elderly most likely to face difficulties due to changing family relationships are residents of villages affected by rural-to-urban migration.

Migration decisions are typically made in the context of the family and with input from different adult family members. Migration is best seen as part of a strategy for the family to cope with economic uncertainty through diversifying its economic resources. But even in cases where a family-based decision is made to send a young adult into the city in search of income, plans do not always pan out the way the family hoped they would. One relevant factor here is the long-term plan of the youth making the move. According to Cai (2003), temporary migrants who are planning to return to their native villages generally remit more money than do those who intend to remain permanently in the city. Furthermore, those with strong family ties (e.g., those who try to return home at least once a year) also remit larger amounts to their parents than do those who don't make these annual visits. Cai interprets these behaviors as aspects of an implicit contractual arrangement between the migrant and the family, whereby the family pools resources to finance the move to the urban center and in turn the migrant is expected to bring money and goods to recompense the family as a whole (Cai 2003:481). Naturally, the degree of responsibility that different migrants feel toward the family they left behind varies, and this variation can be economically and psychologically costly to those on the short end of this stick.

Migration can also disrupt the family's ability to provide a viable support system. For example, it is estimated that 106 million children's lives have been disrupted by parents' search for jobs, with ten million children seldom seeing their parents and another three million never receiving a phone call. Left-behind children are more introverted than their peers, more bullied, and have higher rates of anxiety and depression. The emotional damage is the primary reason for two-thirds of China's juvenile offenders being from rural areas (*Economist* 2015c: 32). The astonishingly rapid growth of cities and the burgeoning incomes this generates have clearly resulted in the disruption of families. And it is the children and the elders left behind who are bearing the emotional burden caused by this disruption (*Economist* 2015c:32).

The migration of young females into the city has resulted in the loss of young women, which is to say daughters and daughters-in-law, from the senior generation's point of view. This has caused serious problems for these elders, given that it is women who most often take on the responsibility of caring for their parents and parents-in-law (Joseph and Philips 1999:153). Many rural families are now being pressed by the consequences of two powerful trends that characterize modern China: economic development that is concentrated mainly in the city, and restrictions on the numbers of children for parents. The loss of young, economically productive offspring in rural areas is placing heavy demands on China's rural elderly that earlier generations never had to face. Given that those in this generation are increasing, partly because of increases in life expectancy (currently about sixty-five years of age), the requirements for home care are growing, particularly in rural areas. The shift to urban living by the young has resulted in an increase in "left-behind" senior citizens who have also become more vulnerable in recent years, not only because of the distress of being left to care for themselves in day-to-day life but also because of an increase in criminal activities. China's National Bureau of Statistics reports that 166 million of the nation's 290 million workers (57 percent) now work in jobs away from their home provinces. Outmigration is particularly common in the most impoverished counties. In one village in Henan in China's interior, 800 of the 1700 villagers are over sixty-five, and 80 percent of them now live alone. Isolated elders like these, unprotected and sometimes overly trusting or confused, are coming to be seen by criminal elements as easy targets (Wang 2012:9).

In spite of all the changes that Chinese families have experienced over the past 120 years, many Confucian values have not entirely disappeared. For example, a remnant of a patrilineal descent ideology continues to be a force in the symbolic arrangements of ritual events (e.g., funerals and marriages), though it has lost much of its significance and power to organize an individual's life strategies. This is especially so among China's singleton generation, in which patrilineal ideology is greatly weakened or entirely gone. Beyond this is the tendency for parents, especially mothers, to take a very lively and sometimes quite forceful role in the choice of spouse for their sons or daughters. But set against these traditional ideals are other social and economic trends. The individual as an autonomous agent, driven more by his or her impulses or interests than by a sense of conventional propriety, is increasingly becoming the new norm for millennial

Chinese. What we see in the Chinese families of today is a wide array of different forms, some of which reflect fairly strong Confucian ideals and in others of which individualism has swept away almost every trace of the patrilineal, patriarchal family system.

In many of these new, post-Confucian families, women insist on rights equal to those enjoyed by their husbands, divorce is almost as likely to end a marriage as is the case in some Western societies, and family members seek to build lives in which they can express themselves as free and individualistic agents. Ultimately, we can say that China presents a greater variety of family forms that respond to a more mixed array of underlying values and political or economic forces than was ever the case before. Beyond this, we can predict that these forms are likely to become more varied and mutable in the future.

Currently China is poised on the brink of a new era in which a powerful, prominent, urban-based middle class stands ready to provide a new impetus to this rapidly developing nation. The families of this middle class have come, more and more, to see themselves as structured in terms of affective bonds. The shift in the marriage ideal has also affected the way offspring view their responsibilities to their parents. They increasingly redefine their relationship away from duty-based filiality toward a relationship based on mutual affection. Marriage is viewed as a partnership where each partner looks first to the needs of his or her spouse, and only secondarily to the needs of their parents.

The social transformation of the Chinese family, then, is intertwined with a reconfiguration of intergenerational bonds and obligations. Although "the normative obligations toward extended kin have diminished, the fact that obligation to parents and extended kin has become more voluntary and discretionary, does not mean that actual contact and help must decline" (Marsh 1996:56). And grandparents continue to play a prominent role in many families. In urban settings, the conjugal family has become the primary family unit, but its monopoly over a child's affection is diluted by the continuing involvement of the senior (or grandparental) generation. The dual multigenerational family continues to serve as a primary reference for the construction of kinship obligations. The persistence with which Chinese grandparents participate in what has become the intergenerational enterprise of raising their only (grand)child is significant. This relationship must be taken into account in any attempt to understand the contemporary Chinese family and urban society. The multigenerational family creates a more supportive environment for both the child and the elderly caretaker. For some individuals it is difficult or impossible, due to outmigration or personal choice, to create a multigenerational or intimate nuclear family support unit. And it is in such cases that the problems of childhood socialization, emotional development, and economic support for elders all come to the fore.

References

Amit, Vered, and Noel Dyck, eds. 2012. *Young Men in Uncertain Times*. New York: Berghahn Books.

Arnett, Jeffrey. 2014. *Emerging Adulthood: The Winding Road from the Late Teens Through the Twenties*. Oxford: Oxford University Press.

Attias-Donfut, Claudine, and Martine Segalen. 2002. "The Construction of Grandparenthood." *Current Sociology* 50(2): 281–94.

Bailey, Beth. 1989. *From Front Porch to Back Seat: Courtship in Twentieth Century America*. Baltimore: Johns Hopkins University Press.

Bian, Yanjie, and John Logan. 1996. "Market Transition and the Persistence of Power: The Changing Stratification System in Urban China." *American Sociological Review* 61: 739–58.

Blake, Fred. 1979a. "Love Songs and the Great Leap: The Role of a Youth Culture in the Revolutionary Phase of China's Economic Development." *American Ethnologist* 6(1): 41–54.

———.1979b. "The Feelings of Chinese Daughters toward Their Mothers as Revealed in Marriage Laments." *Folklore*, 89(2): 91–97.

Brandtstädter, Susanne, and Gonçalo Duro dos Santos, eds. 2009. *Chinese Kinship and Relatedness: Some Contemporary Anthropological Perspectives*. New York: Routledge.

Brockmann, C. Thomas. 1987. "The Western Family and Individuation: Convergence with Caribbean Patterns." *Journal of Comparative Family Studies* 18(3): 471–77.

Burger, Richard. 2013. *Behind the Red Door: Sex in China*. Hong Kong: Earnshaw Ltd.

Burgess, Ernest, and Harvey Locke. 1945. *The Family*. New York: American Book Company.

Buss, David. 2008. *Evolutionary Psychology: The New Science of the Mind* (4th ed.). New York: Routledge.

Cai, Qian. 2003. "Migrant Remittances and Family Ties: A Case Study in China." *International Journal of Population Geography* 9: 471–83.

Carsten, Janet, ed. 2000. "Introduction." In *Cultures of Relatedness*, J. Carsten, ed. Cambridge: Cambridge University Press.

———. 2004. *After Kinship*. Cambridge: Cambridge University Press.

Chan, Kam Wing, and Will Buckingham. 2008. "Is China Abolishing the Hukou System?" *China Quarterly* 2008: 582–606.

Chen, Xinyin, Guohen Cen, Dan Li, and Yunfeng He. 2005. "Social Functioning and Adjustment in Chinese Children: The Imprint of Historical Time." *Child Development* 76: 182–95.

Chen, X., Qiuqiong Huang, Scott Rozelle, Yaojiang Shi, and Linxiu Zhang. 2009. "Effect of Migration on Children's Educational Performance in Rural China." *Comparative Economic Studies* 51: 323–343.

Chang, Leslie. 2009. *Factory Girls: From Village to City in a Changing China*. New York: Spiegel and Grau.

Childs, Geoff. 2003. "Polyandry and Population Growth in a Historical Tibetan Society." *History of the Family* 8: 423–44.

Choi, Yuk-Ping, and Yinni Peng. 2016. *Masculine Compromise: Migration, Family, and Gender in China*. Berkeley: University of California Press.

Chu, Cyrus, and Ruoh-Rong Yu. 2010. *Understanding Chinese Families: A Comparative Study of Taiwan and Southeast China*. Oxford: Oxford University Press.

Chuang, Susan, and Su, Yanjie. 2009. "Do We See Eye to Eye? Chinese Mothers' and Fathers' Parenting Beliefs and Values for Toddlers in Canada and China." *Journal of Family Psychology* 23: 331–41.

Cohen, Myron. 2005a. *Kinship, Contract, Community and State: Anthropological Perspectives on China*. Stanford: Stanford University Press.

———. 2005b. "House United, House Divided: Myths and Realities, Then and Now." In *House, Home, Family: Living and Being Chinese*, R. Knapp, ed. Honolulu: University of Hawaii Press.

———. 1998. "North China Rural Families Changes during the Communist Era." *Etudes Chinoises* 17(1–2): 59–154.

———. 1976. *House United, House Divided: The Chinese Family in Taiwan*. New York: Columbia University Press.

———. 1995. "North China Rural Families Changes during the Communist Era." *Etudes Chinoises* 17(1–2): 59–154.

Collier, Jane. 1997. *From Duty to Desire: Remaking Families in a Spanish Village*. Princeton: Princeton University Press.

Commaille, Jacques. 1983. "Divorce and the Child's Status: The Evolution in France." *Journal of Comparative Family Studies* 14: 97–116.

Cowan, Carolyn, and Philip Cowan. 1992. *When Partners Become Parents: Big Life Changes for Couples*. New York: Basic Books.

Da Marta, Robert. 1979. *Carnivals, Rogues, and Heroes.* Notre Dame: University of Notre Dame Press.

Dautcher, Jay. 2009. *Down a Narrow Road: Identity and Masculinity in a Uyghur Community in Xinjiang, China.* Cambridge: Harvard University Press.

Davis, Deborah. 2014. "Privatization of Marriage in Post-Socialist China." *Modern China* 40 (6): 551–77.

Davis, Deborah, and Sara Friedman. 2014. *Wives, Husbands, and Lovers: Marriage and Sexuality in Hong Kong, Taiwan, and Urban China.* Stanford: Stanford University Press.

Davis, Deborah, and Stevan Harrell. 1993. "Introduction: Impact of Post Mao Reforms on Family Life." In *Chinese Families in the Post Mao Era,* D. Davis and S. Harrell, eds. Berkeley: University of California Press.

Diamant, Neil. 2000. *Revolutionizing the Family: Politics, Love, and Divorce in Urban and Rural China, 1949–1968.* Berkeley: University of California Press.

de Groot, J. J. 1910 / 1982. *The Religious System of the Chinese.* Leyden: E. J. Brill.

Dien, Dora. 1982. "A Chinese Perspective on Kohlberg's Theory of Moral Development." *Developmental Review* 2(4): 331–41.

Dong, Guoli, and Jinping Huang. 2009. "Moral Community: The Imagined Rural Society in 1980s: Interpretation of Movies of Xi Ying Men and Niu Bai Sui." *Journal of East China University of Science and Technology (Social Science Edition)* 1: 28–37.

Dong, Guoli. 2013. "Imagined National State of China in 1980s: An Interpretation of Movie Love on Lushan Mountain." *Journal of East China University of Science and Technology (Social Science Edition)* 5: 1–9.

Dos Santos, Goncalo. 2006. "The Anthropology of Chinese Kinship: A Critical Overview." *European Journal of East Asian Studies* 5(2): 275–333.

———. 2008. "On 'same-year siblings' in rural South China." *Journal of Royal Anthropological Institute* 14: 535–53.

Du, Shanshan. 2002. *"Chopsticks Only Work in Pairs": Gender Unity and Gender Equality among the Lahu of Southwest China.* New York: Columbia University Press.

Engebretsen, Elizabeth. 2016. "Under Pressure: Chinese Lesbian-Gay Contract Marriage and Their Patriarchal Bargains." In *Transformation of Chinese Patriarchy,* S. Harrell and G. dos Santos, eds. Seattle: University of Washington Press.

Economist. 2015a. "China's Left Behind: Little Match Children." October 17.

Economist. 2015b. "Young, Single and What About It?" August 29.

Economist. 2015c. "Bare Branches, Redundant Males." April 18.

Economist. 2011. "Flight from Marriage." August 11.

Evans, Harriet. 2008. *The Subject of Gender: Daughters and Mothers in Urban China*. Lanham: Rowman and Littlefield.

Fan, Cindy, and Youqin Huang. 1998. "Waves of Rural Brides: Female Marriage Migration in China." *Annals of the Association of American Geographers* 88(2): 227–51.

Farrer, James, and Sun Zhongxin. 2003. "Extramarital Love in Shanghai." *The China Journal* 50: 1–36.

Farrer, James. 2014. "Love, Sex, and Commitment: Delinking Premarital Intimacy from Marriage in Urban China." In *Wives, Husbands, and Lovers: Marriage and Sexuality in Hong Kong, Taiwan, and Urban China*, D. S. Davis and S. L. Friedman, eds. Stanford: Stanford University Press.

———. 2010. "A Foreign Adventurer's Parasite? Interracial Sexuality and Alien Sexual Capital in Reform Era Shanghai." *Sexualities* 13(1): 1–27.

———. 2002. *Opening Up: Youth Sex Culture and Market Reform in Shanghai*. Chicago: University of Chicago Press.

Fei, Xiaotung. 1947. *Peasant Life in China: A Field Study of Country Life in the Yangtze Valley*. London: Routledge.

Fisher, Helen. 1992. *Anatomy of Love: The Natural History of Monogamy, Adultery and Divorce*. New York: W. W. Norton.

Fjeld, Heidi. 2005. *Commoners and Nobles: Hereditary Divisions in Tibet*. Copenhagen: NIAS Press.

Fong, Vanessa. 2004. *Only Hope: Coming of Age under China's One-Child Policy*. Stanford: Stanford University Press.

———. 2007. "Parent-Child Communication Problems and the Perceived Inadequacies of Chinese Only Children." *Ethos* 35: 85–127.

———. 2002. "China's One-Child Policy and the Empowerment of Urban Daughters." *American Anthropologist* 104(4): 1098–109.

Freedman, Maurice, 1970. "Ritual Aspects of Chinese Kinship and Marriage." In *Family and Kinship in Chinese Society*, M. Friedman, ed. Stanford: Stanford University Press.

———. 1979. *The Study of Chinese Society*. Stanford: Stanford University Press.

———. 1966. *Chinese Lineage and Society: Fukien and Kwangtung*. London: Athlone Press.

Friedman, Sara. 2006. *Intimate Politics: Marriage, Market and State Power in Southeastern China*. Cambridge: Harvard University Press.

Fung, Heidi. 1999. "Becoming a Moral Child: The Socialization of Shame among Young Chinese Children." *Ethos* 27(2):180–209.

Gallin, Bernie, and Rita Gallin. 1997. "Sociopolitical Power and Sworn Brother Groups in Chinese Society: A Taiwanese Case." In *Anthropology of Power*, R. D. Fogelson and R. N. Adams, eds. New York: Academic Press.

Gaetano, Arianne, and Tarma Jacka. 2004. *On the Move: Women and Rural to Urban Migration in Contemporary China*. New York: Columbia University Press.

Gauthier, Anne. 2002. "The Role of Grandparents." *Current Sociology* 50(2): 295–307.

Giddens, Anthony. 1992. *The Transformation of Intimacy: Sexuality, Love and Eroticism in Modern Societies*. Cambridge: Polity.

Goh, Esther. 2006. "Raising the Precious Single Child in Urban China: An Intergenerational Joint Mission Between Parents and Grandparents." *Journal of Intergenerational Relationships* 4(3): 6–23.

Goode, William. 1963. *World Revolution and Family Patterns*. New York: The Free Press.

Gold, Tom. 1985. "After Comradeship: Personal Relations in China Since the Cultural Revolution." *China Quarterly*, 104: 657–75.

Goldstein, Melvyn. 1971. "Stratification, Polyandry, and Family Structure in Central Tibet." *Southwestern Journal of Anthropology* 27: 64–74.

———. 1987. "When Brothers Share a Wife." *Natural History* March: 39–48.

Goldstein, Melvyn, Ben Jiao, Cynthia Beall, and Phuntsok Tsering. 2002. "Fertility and Family Planning in Rural Tibet." *The China Journal* 47(1): 19–39.

Goodman, Bryna. 1995. *Native Place, City, and Nation, Regional Networks and Identities in Shanghai, 1853–1937*. Berkeley: University of California Press.

Gottlieb, Beatrice. 1993. *The Family In the Western World*. New York: Oxford University Press.

Granovetter, Mark. 1973. "The Strength of Weak Ties." *American Journal of Sociology* 78(6): 1360–80.

Greenhalgh, Susan. 2013. "Patriarchal Demographics: China's Sex Ratio Reconsidered." *Population and Development Review* 38(1): 130–49.

Hall, David. 1996. "Marriage as a Pure Relationship: Exploring the Link Between Premarital Cohabitation and Divorce in Canada." *Journal of Comparative Family Studies* 27(1): 1–12.

Hanan, Patrick. 1988. *The Invention of Li Yu*. Cambridge: Cambridge University Press.

Hansen, Mette, and Cuiming Pang. 2008. "Me and My Family: Perceptions of Individual and Collective among Youth Rural Chinese." *European Journal of East Asian Studies* 7(1): 75–99.

Harrell, Stevan. 2001. "Anthropology of China." *Annual Reviews in Anthropology* 30: 139–61.

He, Dan. 2014. "Government Seeks Ways to Reverse Worrying Rise in Divorce Rate," *China Daily On-line*, March 24.

Hershatter, Gail. 1992. *Dangerous Pleasures: Prostitution and Modernity in Twentieth-Century Shanghai.* Berkeley: University of California Press.

Hinsch, Bret. 1990. *Passions of the Cut Sleeve: The Male Homosexual Tradition in China.* Berkeley: University of California Press.

Hinton, Carmen, and Robert Gordon. 1984. *Small Happiness* (a film).

Ho, David. 1987. "Fatherhood in Chinese Society." In M. Lamb, ed. *The Father's Role: Cross-Cultural Perspective.* Hilldale: Lawrence Erlbaum.

Honig, Emily, and Gail Hershatter. 1988. *Personal Voices: Chinese Women in the 1980's.* Stanford: Stanford University Press.

Hong, Xiao. 2000. "The Structure of Child-Rearing Values in Urban China." *Sociological Perspectives* 43(3): 457–71.

Hsiung, Ping-Chien. 2005. *A Tender Voyage: Children and Childhood in Late Imperial China.* Stanford: Stanford University Press.

Hsu, Elisabeth. 1998. "Moso and Naxi: The House." In *Naxi and Moso Ethnography: Kin, Rites, Pictographs*, M. Oppitz and E. Hsu, eds. Zurich: Völkerkundesmuseum.

Hu, W., J. Gao, T. Kang, B. Wu, K. Shi, X. Wang, and Z. Wen. 2009. "Research on the Relationship and Influencing Factors between University Students' Empathy and Parental Rearing Patterns." *China Journal of Health Psychology*: 1050–55.

Hui, Nu. 2013. "Temporary Marriages." *Tea Leaf Nation* 27: 1–3.

Ikels, Charlotte. 2004. "The Impact of Housing Policy on China's Urban Elderly." *Urban Anthropology* 33 (2–4): 321–355.

Jacka, Tarma. 2012. "Migration, House Holding and the Well-Being of Left-Behind Women in Rural Ningxia." *China Journal* 67: 1–21.

———. 2006. *Rural Women in Urban China: Gender: Migration and Social Change.* Amonk: M. E. Sharpe.

Jankowiak, William. 2013. "From Courtship to Dating Culture: China's Emergent Youth." In *Restless China*, P. Link, R. P. Madsen, and P. G. Pickowicz, eds. Lanham: Rowman and Littlefield.

———. 2011. "The Han Chinese Family: The Realignment of Parenting Ideals, Sentiments, and Practices." In *Women and Gender in Contemporary Chinese Societies*, S. Du and Y. Chen, eds. Lexington: Rowman & Littlefield Publishers.

———. 2009. "Practicing Connectiveness as Kinship in Urban China." In *Chinese Kinship and Relatedness: Some Contemporary Anthropological Perspectives*, S. Brandstader and G. dos Santos, eds. New York: Routledge.

————. 2006. "Gender, Power, and the Denial of Intimacy in Chinese Studies and Beyond." *Reviews in Anthropology* 35(4): 305–24.

————. 2004. "Well Being, Family Affections, and Ethical Nationalism in Urban China." *Urban Anthropology and Studies of Cultural Systems and World Economic Development* 33 (2–4).

————. 1993. *Sex, Death, and Hierarchy in a Chinese City*. New York: Columbia University Press.

————. 1992. "Father-Child Relations in Urban China." In Barry S. Hewlett, ed., *Father-Child Relations: Cultural and Biosocial Contexts*. New York: Aldine Press.

Jankowiak, William, and Edward Fischer. 1992. "A Cross-Cultural Perspective on Romantic Love." *Ethnology* 31(2): 149–55.

Jankowiak, William, and Xuan Li. 2016. "Emergent Conjugal Love, Male Affection, and Female Power". In *Is Chinese Patriarchy Over? The Decline and Transformation of a System of Social Support*, Stevan Harrell and Goncalo dos Santos, eds. Seattle: Washington University Press. (In press).

Jankowiak, William, Robert Moore, and Tianshu Pan. 2012. "Institutionalizing an Extended Youth Phase in Chinese Society: Social Class and Sex Differences in the Pursuit of the Personal and the Pragmatic." In *Young Men in Uncertain Times*, V. Amit and N. Dyck, eds. New York: Berghahn Books.

Jankowiak, William, and Thomas Paladino. 2008. "Desiring Sex, Longing for Love." In *Intimacies: Love and Sex Across Cultures*, W. Jankowiak, ed. New York: Columbia University Press.

Johnson, Kay. 2016. *China's Hidden Children: Abandonment, Adoption, and the Human Cost of the One-Child Policy*. Chicago: University of Chicago Press.

————. 1983. *Women, the Family and Peasant Revolution in China*. Chicago: University of Chicago Press.

Jones, Andrew. 1992. *Like a Knife: Ideology and Genre in Contemporary Chinese Popular Music*. Ithaca: Cornell East Asia Series.

Joseph, Alun, and D. R. Philips. 1999. "Aging in Rural China: Impacts of Increasing Diversity in Family and Community Resources." *Journal of Cross Cultural Gerontology* 14: 153–68.

Jordan, David. 1985. "Sworn Brothers: A Study in Ritual Kinship." In *Chinese Family and Its Ritual Behavior*, J.-C. Hsieh and Y.-C. Chuang, eds. Taipei: Academia Sinica.

Judd, Ellen. 2009. "Families We Create: Women's Kinship in Rural China as Spatialized Practice." In *Chinese Kinship and Relatedness: Some Contemporary Anthropological Perspectives*, S. Brandstader and G. D. dos Santos, eds. New York: Routledge.

Kam, Louie. 2013. *Shanghai Lalas: Female Tongzhi Communities and Politics in Urban China*. Hong Kong University Press.

Khan, Usman, Alexander L. N. van Nuijs, Jing Li, Walid Maho, Peng Du, Kaiyang Li, Linlin Hou, Jiying Zhang, Xhiangzhou Meng, Xiqing Li, and Adrian Covaci. 2014. "Application of a Sewage-Based Approach to Assess the Use of Ten Illicit Drugs in Four Chinese Megacities." *Science of the Total Environment* 487: 710–21.

Kim, Won Sung, Vanessa Fong, Hirokazu Yoshikawa, Niobe Way, Xinyin Chen, Hui Hua Deng, and Zuhong Lu. 2010. "Income, Work Preferences and Gender Roles Among Parents of Infants in Urban China: A Mixed Method Study from Nanjing." *China Quarterly* 204: 939–61.

Kim, Won Sung, and Vanessa Fong. 2014. "A Longitudinal Study of Son and Daughter Preference Among Chinese Only-Children From Adolescence to Adulthood." *The China Journal* 71: 1–24.

Kipnis, Andrew. 1997. *Producing Guanxi: Sentiment, Self, and Subculture in a North China Village*. Durham: Duke University Press.

Kuan, Teresa. 2011. "'The Heart Says One Thing But The Hand Does Another': A Story About Emotion-Work, Ambivalence and Popular Advice for Parents." *The China Journal* 65: 82–101.

Kwok, Sylvia, Sylvia Ling Chloe, Cyrus Leung, and Jessica Li. 2013. "Fathering Self-Efficacy, Marital Satisfaction and Father Involvement in Hong Kong." *Journal of Childhood Family Studies*, 22:1051–1060.

Lamb, M. E. (Ed.). (1987). *The Father's Role: Cross-Cultural Perspectives*. Hillsdale, NJ: Lawrence Erlbaum Associates.

Lang, Olga. 1945. *Chinese Family and Society*. New Haven: Yale University.

Lawton, Leona, Merril Silverstein, and Vern Bengtson. 1994. "Solidarity Between Generations in Families." In *Intergenerational Linkages: Hidden Connections in American Society*, V. Bengtson and R. Hasrootyan, eds. New York: Springer Publishing.

Lee, Ching Kuan. 1998. *Gender and the South China Miracle*. Berkeley: University of California Press.

Lee, Sing, and Arthur Kleinman. 2003. "Suicide as Resistance." In *Chinese Society: Change, Conflict and Resistance*, 2nd ed, E. Perry and M. Seldon, eds. London: Routledge.

Lee, Haiyan. 2010. *Revolution of the Heart: A Genealogy of Love in China, 1900–1950*. Stanford: Stanford University Press.

Levin, David. 2013. "Festival's Resurgence Has Chinese Sending Manna to the Heavens." *New York Times*, April 4.

Levine, Nancy. 1988. *The Dynamics of Polyandry: Kinship, Domesticity, and Population on the Tibetan Border*. Chicago: University of Chicago Press.

Levy, Marion. 1949/1968. *Family Revolution in Modern China*. Cambridge: Harvard University Press; repr. New York: Atheneum Press.

———. 1950. *Family Revolution in Modern China*. Cambridge: Harvard University Press.

Li, Sun, and Meidong Hu. 2014. "The Price of Marriage." *China Daily*, July 13.

Li, Xuan, and Michael Lamb. 2013. "Fathers in Chinese Culture: From Stern Disciplinarians to Involved Parents." In *Fathers in Cultural Context*, D. Swalb, B. J. Swalb, and M. Lamb, eds. New York: Routledge.

Li, X.Y., Michael Philips, Y. P. Zhang, D. Xu, and G. H. Yang. 2008. Risk Factors for Suicide in China's Youth: A Case-Control Study. *Psychological Medicine* 38(3): 397–406.

Lindholm, Charles. 2001. *Culture and Identity*. New York: McGraw Hill.

Liang, Heng, and Judith Shapiro. 1983. *Son of the Revolution*. New York: Knopf.

Link, Perry. 1981. *Mandarin Ducks and Butterflies: Popular Fiction in Early Twentieth-Century Chinese Cities*. Berkeley: University of California Press.

Liu, Fengshu. 2011. *Urban Youth in China: Modernity, the Internet and the Self*. New York: Routledge.

———. 2008. "Negotiating the Filial Self: Young Adult Only Children and Intergenerational Relationships in China." *Young* 16(4): 409–30.

Liu, Xin. 2000. *In One's Own Shadow: An Ethnographic Account of the Condition of Post-Reform Rural China*. Berkeley: University of California Press.

Louie, Kam. 2000. *Chinese Masculinity*. Cambridge: Cambridge University Press.

Lu, Huijing, and Lei Chang. 2013. "Parenting and Socialization of Only Children in Urban China: An Example of Authoritative Parenting." *The Journal of Genetic Psychology* 174(3): 335–43.

Lu, Melody, and Wensha Yang, eds. 2010. *Asian Cross Border Marriage Migration*. Amsterdam: Amsterdam University Press.

Lytton, Hugh, and David Romney. 1991. "Parents' Differential Socialization of Boys and Girls: A Meta-Analysis." *Psychological Bulletin*: 267–296.

Mason, Katherine. 2016. *Infectious Change: Reinventing Chinese Public Health after an Epidemic*. Stanford: Stanford University Press.

Marsh, Robert. 1996. *The Great Transformation: Social Change in Taibei*. Armonk, N.Y.: M.E. Sharpe.

Mischel, Walter. 1958. "Preference for Delayed Reinforcement: An Experimental Study of a Cultural Observation." *Journal of Abnormal and Social Psychology* 56: 57–61.

Mintz, Steven. 2004. *Huck's Raft: A History of American Childhood*. Cambridge: Harvard University Press.

Moore, Robert, and Li Wei. 2012. "Modern Love in China," in *The Psychology of Love*, Vol. 3, Michele Paludi, ed. Santa Barbara, California: Praeger.

Moore, Robert. 2015. "Like the Air We Breathe: Confucianism and Chinese Youth," in *The Sage Returns: Confucian Revival in Contemporary China*, Kenneth J. Hammond and Jeffrey L. Richey, eds. Albany: SUNY Press.

———. 2005. "Generation Ku: Individualism and China's Millennial Youth." *Ethnology* 44: 357–76.

———. 1998. "Love and Limerence with Chinese Characteristics: Student Romance in the PRC," in *Romantic Love and Sexual Behavior: Perspectives from the Social Sciences*, Victor C. De Munck, ed. Westport, Conn.: Praeger.

Moore, Robert and James Rizor. 2008. "Confucian and Cool: China's Youth in Transition." *Education About Asia* 13(3): 30–7.

Moore, Robert, Eric Bindler, and David Pandich. 2010. "Language with Attitude: American Slang and Chinese *Liyu*," *Journal of Sociolinguistics* 14 (4): 524–38, Fall.

Mattison, Siobhan, Scelza Booke, and Tami Blumenfield. 2014. "Paternal Investment and the Positive Effects of Fathers among the Matrilineal Mosuo of Southwest China." *American Anthropologist* 116(3): 591–610.

Myerson, Rebecca, Yubo Hou, Huizhen Tang, Ying Cheng, Ying Ye, and Ying Wang. 2010. "Home and Away: Chinese Migrant Workers Between Two Worlds." *The Sociological Review* 58: 29–39.

McKann, Charles. 1998. "Naxi, Rerkua, Moso, Meng: Kinship, Politics and Ritual on the Yunnan-Sichuan Frontier," in *Naxi and Moso Ethnography: Kin, Rites, Pictographs*, Michael Oppitz and Elizabeth Hsu, eds., Zurich: Völkerkundesmuseum.

Naftali, Orna. 2010. "Caged Golden Canaries: Childhood, Privacy, and Subjectivity in Contemporary Urban China." *Childhood* 17(3): 297–311.

———. 2009. "Empowering the Child: Children's Rights, Citizenship, and the State in Contemporary China." *The China Journal*. No. 61:79–104.

Nye, Robert. 2000. "Friendship, Male Bonds, and Masculinity in Perspective." *American Historical Review*: 1656–70.

Onnis, Barbara. 2012. "The Scourge of Prostitution in Contemporary China: The 'Bao Ernai' Phenomenon." *Asian Culture and History* 4(2): 91–98.

Osburg, John. 2013. *Anxious Wealth: Money and Morality among China's New Rich*. Stanford: Stanford University Press.

Ottenheimer, Martin. 1996. *Forbidden Relatives: The American Myth of Cousin Marriage*. Urbana: University of Illinois Press.

Oxfeld, Ellen. 2010. *Drink Water, but Remember the Source: Moral Discourse in a Chinese Village*. Stanford: Stanford University Press.

Potter, Sulamith, and Jack Potter. 1990. *China's Peasants: The Anthropology of a Revolution*. Cambridge: Cambridge University Press.

Rudelson, Justin, and William Jankowiak. 2004. "Acculturation and Resistance," in *Xinjiang: China's Muslim Borderland*, S. Frederick Starr, ed. 318–32. Armonk, N.Y.: M.E. Sharpe.

Parish, William, Wang Tianfu, Edward Laumann, Suming Pan, and Ye Luo. 2004. "Intimate Partner Violence in China: National Prevalence, Risk Factors, and Associate Health Problems." *International Family Planning Perspectives* 30(4): 174–81.

Parish, William, and Martin Whyte. 1978. *Village and Family in Contemporary China*. Chicago: University of Chicago Press.

Parsons, Talcott. 1964 (original 1951). *The Social System*. New York: Free Press.

Penglase, R. 2014. *Living with Insecurity in a Brazilian Favela*. New Brunswick: Rutgers University Press.

People's Daily. 2011. "Home-Hidden Crime Scenes." *People's Daily*, Nov. 4: 1–2.

Pickowicz, Paul, and Liping Wang. 2002. "Village Voices, Urban Activists: Women, Violence, and Gender Inequality in Rural China," in *Popular China: Unofficial Culture in a Globalizing Society*, Perry Link, Richard P. Madsen, and Paul G. Pickowicz, eds. New York: Rowman and Littlefield.

Potter, Sulthmin. 1988. "The Cultural Construction of Emotion in Rural Chinese Social Life." *Ethos* 16(2): 181–208.

Putnick, Diane, Marc Bornstein, Jennifer Lansford, Lei Chang, Kirby Deater-Deckard, Laura Di Giunta, Sevtap Gurdal, Kenneth Dodge, Patrick Malone, Paul Oburu, Concetta Pastorelli, Ann Skinner, Emma Sorbring, Sombat Tapanya, Liliana Tirado, Arnaldo Zelli, Liane Alampay, Suha Al-Hassan, Dario Bacchini, and Anna Bombi. 2012. "Agreement in Mother and Father Acceptance, Rejection, Warmth, and Hostility/Rejection/ Neglect of Children Across Nine Countries." *Cross-Cultural Research* 46(3): 191–223.

Pye, Lucian. 1985. *Asian Power and Politics*. Cambridge: Harvard University Press.

Santos, Goncalo. 2006. "The Anthropology of Chinese Kinship: A Critical Overview." *European Journal of East Asian Studies* 5(2): 275–333.

———. 2016. "Multiple Mothering and Labor Migration in Rural South China," in Gonçalo Santos and Stevan Harrell, eds., *Transforming Patriarchy: Chinese Families in the 21st Century*. Seattle and London: University of Washington Press.

Schlegel, Alice, and Herbert Barry. 1983. *Adolescence*. New York: Free Press.

Schneider, Melissa. 2014. *The Ugly Wife Is a Treasure at Home*. Lincoln, Neb.: Potomac.

Shaw, Thomas. 1994. " 'We like to have fun': Leisure and the Discovery of the Self in Taiwan's New Middle Class." *Modern China* 20(4): 416–45.

Shen Yifei. 2013. *Geti Jiatingi Family: Zhongguo Chengshi Xiandaihua Jincheng Zhong De Geti Jiating Yu Guojia*. Shanghai: Shanghai Sanlian Chubanshe.

———. 2009. "China in the Post-Patriarchal Era: Changes In The Power Relationships Within Urban Households and an Analysis of the Course of Gender Inequality in Society." *Chinese Sociology and Anthropology*, 43(4): 5–23.

Shih, Chuan-kang. 2010. *Quest for Harmony: The Moso Traditions of Sexual Union and Family Life*. Stanford: Stanford University Press.

———. 2001. "Genesis of Marriage among the Moso and Empire-Building in Late Imperial China," *Journal of Asian Studies* 60(2): 381–412.

Shi, Lihong. 2017. *Choosing Daughters: Family Change in Rural China*. Stanford: Stanford University Press.

———. 2016. "From Care Provider to Financial Burden: The Changing Role of Sons and Reproductive Choice in Rural Northeast China." In *Transforming Chinese Patriarchy: Chinese Families in the 21st Century*, G. dos Santos and S. Harrell, eds. Seattle: University of Washington Press.

———. 2011. " 'The Wife Is The Boss' ": Sex-Ratio Imbalance And Young Women's Empowerment In Rural Northeast China." In *Women and Gender in Contemporary Chinese Societies*, S. Du and Y. Chen, eds. Lexington: Rowman & Littlefield Publishers.

———. 2009. "Little Quilted Vests To Warm Parents' Hearts: Redefining The Gendered Practice Of Filial Piety In Rural North-Eastern China." *China Quarterly*: 348–65.

Short, S., Zhai Fengying, Xu Siyuan, and Yang Mingliang. 2001. "China's One-Child Policy and the Care of Children: An Analysis of Qualitative and Quantitative Data." *Social Forces* 79(3): 913–43.

Shulman, Shmuel, and Mosha, Klein. 1993. "The Distinctive Role of the Father in Adolescent Separation-Individuation." *New Directions for Child Development* 62: 41–58.

Shwalb, D., B. J. Shwalb, and M. Lamb, eds. 2013. *Fathers in Cultural Context*. New York: Routledge.

Smart, Alan. 1999. "Expressions Of Interest: Friendship and Guanxi in Chinese Societies." In *The Anthropology of Friendship*, S. Bell and S. Coleman, eds. Oxford: Berg.

Solinger, D. 1999. *Contesting Citizenship in Urban China: Peasant Migration, the State and the Logic of the Market*. Berkeley: University of California Press.

Solomon, Richard. 1971. *Mao's Revolution and Chinese Political Culture*. Berkeley: University of California Press.

Sommer, Matthew. 2015. *Polyandry and Wife-Selling in Qing Dynasty China*. Stanford: Stanford University Press.

Song, Sophie. 2013. "Chinese Mistress Culture 101: The Difference Between an Ernai and a Xiaosan," *International Business Times*, Oct. 11, 2013.

Stafford, Charles. 2000. "Chinese Patriliny and the Cycles of Yang and Laiwang." In *Cultures of Relatedness*, J. Carsten, ed. Cambridge: Cambridge University Press.

———. 1995. *Roads to Chinese Parenthood*. Cambridge, UK: Cambridge University Press.

Stockard, Janet. 1989. *Daughters of the Canton Delta: Marriage Patterns and Economic Strategies in South China, 1860–1930*. Stanford: Stanford University Press.

Strom, R. D., Strom, S. K., and Xie, Q. 1995. "The Small Family in China." *International Journal of Early Childhood*, 27(2): 37–45.

Sun, Yuezhu. 2013. "Among a Hundred Good Virtues Filial Piety Is the First: Moral Discourses in Contemporary Urban China." Paper delivered at the American Anthropological Association, Chicago.

Szonyi, Michael. 2002. *Practicing Kinship: Lineage and Descent in Late Imperial China*. Stanford: Stanford University Press.

Tam, Vicky, and Raymond Chan. 2009. "Parental Involvement with Primary Children's Homework." *School Community Journal*, 19(2): 81–100.

Tang, Tianfu, and William Parish. 2000. *Urban Life Under Reform*. Cambridge: Cambridge University Press.

Thornton, Arland, William Axinn, and Yu Xie. 2007. *Marriage and Cohabitation*. Chicago: University of Chicago Press.

Tien, Ju-k'ang. 1988. *Male Anxiety and Female Chastity: A Comparative Study of Chinese Ethical Values in Ming Ch'ing Times*. Leiden: Brill.

Unger, Jon. 1993. "Urban Families in the Eighties: An Analysis of Chinese Surveys." In *Chinese Families in the Post Mao Era*, Deborah Davis and Stevan Harrell, eds. Berkeley: University of California Press.

Wang, Xiaoqi. 2012. "Protect Vulnerable Senior Citizens." *China Daily*, July 4: 9.

Waley, Arthur, trans., 1938. *The Analects of Confucius*, trans. and ann. by Arthur Waley. New York: Random House.

———. 1960. *The Book of Songs: The Ancient Chinese Classic of Poetry*. New York: Grove Weidenfeld.

Waller, William. 1937. "The Rating and Dating Complex," *American Sociological Review* 2: 720–34.

Watson, James, and Rubie Watson. 2004. *Village Life in Hong Kong: Politics, Gender, and Ritual in the New Territories*. Hong Kong: Chinese University Press.

Watson, Rubie. 2007. "Families in China: Ties that Bind." Paper for The Family Model in Chinese Art and Culture Conference Princeton University, Nov. 6–7, 2004.

Watson, R. 1985. *Inequality Amongst Brothers: Class and Kinship in South China.* Cambridge: Cambridge University Press.

Way, Niobe, Sumie Okazaki, Jing Zhao, Joanna J. Kim, Xinyin Chen, Hirokazu Yoshikawa, Yueming Jia, and Huihua Deng. 2013. "Social and Emotional Parenting: Mothering in a Changing Chinese Society." *Asian American Journal of Psychology* 4(1): 61–70.

Wen, Chihua. 1995. *The Red Mirror: Children of China's Cultural Revolution.* Bruce Jones, ed., pp. 97–112. Boulder, CO: Westview Press.

Whyte, Martin, Wang Feng, and Yong Cai. 2015. "Challenging Myths about China's One-Child Policy." *The China Journal*, No.74: 144–159.

Whyte, Martin. 2005. "Continuity and Change in Urban Chinese Family Life." *China Journal* 53: 9–33.

———. 1997. "The Fate of Filial Obligations in Urban China." *China Journal* 38: 1–31.

Whyte, Martin, and William Parish. 1984. *Urban Life in Contemporary China.* Chicago: University of Chicago Press.

Wilson, Richard. 1974. "The Moral State: A Study of the Political Socialization of Chinese and American Children." *Normal and Abnormal Behavior in Chinese Culture.* Arthur Kleinman and Tsung-Yi Lin eds. pp. 124–36. Holland: Reidel.

Wolf, Arthur. 1995. *Sexual Attraction: Legal Brief for Westermarck.* Stanford: Stanford University Press.

Wolf, Margery. 1972. *Women and the Family in Rural Taiwan.* Stanford: Stanford University Press.

Wong, Edward. 2014. "Weighing in on Paid Interethnic Marriages in Xinjiang," *New York Times*, September 5.

———. 2013. "Filial Piety, Once a Virtue in China, Is Now the Law." *New York Times*, July 2: 3.

Wu, Benxue. 1987. "The Urban Family in Flux." In *New Trends in Chinese Marriage and the Family.* Beijing: China International Book Trading.

Xu, Gary, and Susan Feiner. 2007. "*Meinü Jingji*/China's Beauty Economy: Buying Looks, Shifting Value and Changing Place," *Feminist Economics* 13(3–4): 307–23.

Xu, Jing. 2014. "Becoming a Moral Child amidst China's Moral Crisis: Preschool Discourse and Practices of Sharing in Shanghai." *Ethos* 42: 222–42.

Xu, Xiaohe, and Martin Whyte. 1990. "Love Matches and Arranged Marriages: A Chinese Replication." *Journal of Marriage and the Family* 52: 709–22.

Xu, Y., and L. Zhang. 2008. "Rural Fathers' Will, Acts and Experience of Parenting: Experienced Researcher of Shanghai Suburbs." *Hunan Normal University Bulletin*, 3: 72–76.

Xue Zhao, Jian Chen, Ming-Chun Chen, Xiao-Ling Lv, Yu-Hong Jiang, and Ye-Huan Sun. 2014. "Left-Behind Children in Rural China Experience Higher Levels of Anxiety and Poorer Living Conditions." *Acta Paediatrica* 103: 665–70.

Yan, Ruxian. 1986. *Zhongguo shaoshuminzu hunyin jiating Beijing: Zhongguo funu* (in Mandarin).

Yan, Ruxian, and Song Zhaolin. 1983. *The Natrilineal System of the Yongning Naxi* (in Mandarin). Kunming: Yunnan renmin Chubanshe.

Yan, Yunxiang. 2010. "Chinese Path to Individuation." *The British Journal of Sociology* 61(3): 489–512.

———. 2009. *The Individualization of Chinese Society*, Vol. 77 of the London School of Economics Monographs on Social Anthropology. Oxford: Berg Publishers.

———. 2005. "The Individual and Transformation of Bridewealth in Rural North China." *Journal of the Royal Anthropological Institute* 11(4): 637–58.

———. 2003. *Private Life under Socialism: Love, Intimacy, and Family Change in a Chinese Village*. Stanford: Stanford University Press.

———. 1999. "Rural Youth and Youth Culture in North China," *Culture, Medicine and Psychiatry* 23(1): 75–97.

———. 1997. "The Triumph of Conjugality: Structural Transformation of Family Relations in a Chinese Village." *Ethnology* 36(3):191–212.

———. 1996. *Flow of Gifts*. Stanford: Stanford University Press.

Yang, Kelly. 2013. "In China, it's the Grandparents Who 'Lean In'". *The Atlantic*, Sept. 30: 1–10.

Yang, Martin. 1994. "Reshaping Peasant Culture and Community: Rural Industrialization in a Chinese Village." *Modern China* 20(2): 157–79.

Yuen, Sun-pong, Pui-lam Law, and Yuk-ying Ho. 2004. *Marriage, Gender, and Sex in a Contemporary Chinese Village*. Trans. Fong-ying Yu. Armonk, N.Y.: Sharpe.

Yue, Daiyun, and Carol Wakeman. 1985. *To the Storm: The Odyssey of a Revolutionary Chinese Woman*. Berkeley: University of California Press.

Zhang, F. 2009. "A Study on Satisfaction Degree on the Father Image by Middle School Parents." *Journal of Taiyuan Normal University (Social Science Edition)*, 8(4):18–20.

Zhang, Hong. 2006. "Family Care or Residential Care? The Moral and Practical Dilemmas Facing the Elderly in Urban China." *Asian Anthropology* 5 (2006): 57–83.

———. 2005. "Bracing for an Uncertain Future." *China Journal* 64: 85.

Zhang, Jie. 1986 [orig. 1979] "Love Must Not Be Forgotten," in *Love Must Not Be Forgotten*. San Francisco: China Books and Periodicals.

Zang, Xiaowei. 2007. *Ethnicity and Urban Life in China*. New York: Routledge.

———. 2012. *Islam, Family Life, and Gender Inequality in Urban China*. New York: Routledge.

Zhang, Yan. 2011. "More Women Kidnapped for Brides," *China Daily* Dec. 3, 2011.

Zheng, Tiantian. 2015. *Tongzhi Living*. Minneapolis: University of Minneapolis Press.

Zuo, Jiping. 2009. "Rethinking Family Patriarchy and Women's Positions in Presocialist China." *Journal of Marriage and Family* 71: 542–57.

Index